Claire Austin's
Book of
PERENNIALS

Claire Austin

White Hopton Publications

Published in 2015 by White Hopton Publications
Newtown, Powys SY16 4EN

Design, text, photography copyright © Claire Austin 2015

Claire Austin has asserted her right to be identified as author
of this work in accordance with the Copyright, Designs and
Patents Act, 1988.

A CIP catalogue record for this book is available from the
British Library.

ISBN 978-0-9931647-0-5

Project managed and edited for White Hopton Publications
by:
OutHouse Publishing
Winchester, Hampshire SO22 5DS
Project manager Sue Gordon
Editor Anna Kruger
Proofreader Jo Weeks
Indexer Marie Lorimer

Print management by Peter Dane
Printhouse, pdane@printhouseltd.co.uk

Printed and bound in Great Britain using materials
accredited by the Forest Stewardship Council® by
Pureprint Group
Uckfield, East Sussex TN22 1PL
www.pureprint.com

Front cover *Sanguisorba* 'Pink Tanna'
Back cover *Centaurea* 'Blewitt' with *Astrantia major* 'Claret'

Claire Austin Hardy Plants,
White Hopton Farm, Wern Lane, Sarn, Newtown SY16 4EN
www.claireaustin-hardyplants.co.uk

Contents

A border filled with a varied selection of hardy perennials at White Hopton Farm, July

The gazebo at White Hopton is a perfect place to sit and enjoy the garden

MY PASSION FOR PERENNIALS

Perennials have been a passion of mine for over 30 years. During this time I have grown them on my nursery and planted them in my seven different gardens. Although not a trained garden designer, I have used perennials to paint the picture each garden demanded. They offer so much: colour, shape, texture, flowers for the house, and they also invite nature in.

My first book about perennials was written in 1999, commissioned as a result of the colourful catalogue we produced for the nursery each year. The catalogue eventually ran to hundreds of pages, which wasn't cost effective. With rising internet sales, our focus has now shifted to selling plants through the website rather than via our catalogue, which is now much smaller.

However, frustrated by my own online research into more unusual perennials and following repeated requests from customers for the old catalogue, as well as for copies of my first book (long out of print), I realised that there was still a need for a practical, highly illustrated guide to perennials. And so I wrote this book, which is designed not as a selling guide but to encourage all gardeners, especially new ones, to try perennials. The range of plants in the Plant Directory is far from exhaustive, but these are all perennials I have grown and found to be reliable. It is a personal selection and I make no apologies for ignoring your favourites. *Solidago*, for example, I have no time for, while treasures such as *Trachystemon* aren't included because they aren't readily available.

The introductory section describes how I grow perennials and combine them in the garden. In my early years of growing perennials, I found inspiration in the pages of Graham Stuart Thomas's book *Perennial Garden Plants* (Dent, 1976). I grew up knowing Graham. He was never without a small notebook, which he carried in his pocket. If he saw anything interesting he would jot it down. My notebook is my camera. All the pictures in this book were taken by me in my gardens – most of them in the garden at White Hopton Farm.

WHY GROW PERENNIALS?

Of all the plant groups, perennials are the most versatile. They grow in all soils from dry to wet, and in conditions from full sun through to shade. In size and shape, they can form a ground-hugging carpet or a clump that is head-high. In terms of flower colour, there are perennials in every shade from white to almost black, and they have a fabulous range of forms and textures. Most importantly, they are usually very easy to grow, filling a border quickly with leaves and flowers from early spring to late autumn. Some are even generous enough to provide flowers in winter. In short, there can be no doubt that perennials deserve pride of place in every garden.

White Hopton Farm garden, September

The term perennial describes any plant that lives for more than two years. It includes trees, shrubs, and bulbs, as well as herbaceous perennials – the subject of this book. In the wild, perennials are found in all parts of the world, although many are not full hardy in this country. While they grow to all sizes, many of the smallest perennials need specific growing conditions, and for gardening purposes these fall into a separate group – alpines. The plants that inspire me, and that feature in this book, are hardy herbaceous perennials. They are very diverse, tolerate a wide range of soils and situations, and are ideal for flower beds or borders.

CHOOSING THE RIGHT PERENNIALS

Over the past 30 years I have grown hundreds of different perennial varieties. Many are still available, some have disappeared. Today, the range of plants may have increased, but choosing them has not become any easier. At one time, plants were bought from nurseries or through catalogues from nurserymen who could offer advice. Now, when online sales of plants are increasing, advice is hard to come by, although you may get some information from stands at a show or a garden centre. Often, however, the plants on display are simply those that are looking good at that particular moment – and may also be part of a special promotion. These may not the best plants for your garden. In this section of the book you'll find guidance on choosing the right plants for the soil and aspect of your particular plot.

Once there were hundreds of *Aster* varieties. Without the work of National Collection holders, many more might have disappeared

Around 30 years ago, there were very few varieties of *Astrantia*; *A. maxima* was one of them

Introduced just after World War II by George Russell, lupins have always been popular

New *Echinacea* hybrids are popping up everywhere. Many are bred in the USA and Holland, but not all are hardy or long-lived

NAMING PERENNIALS

I feel strongly that plants should be known by their Latin (botanical) name rather than the common name. The convention is to put the Latin name in italics, such as *Achillea*, followed by the common name in brackets (yarrow). Latin names are a combination of botanical terminology, and a descriptive or given name, which is within inverted commas, for example *Achillea* 'Terracotta'. These are not always the easiest words to pronounce or spell, but they are an international language, and their use saves confusion, particularly as common names vary throughout the world. Bluebell, for example, is the common name of our familiar spring bulb, *Hyacinthoides non-scripta*, whereas in North America, a bluebell is a woodland perennial, *Mertensia virginica*.

TRADE NAMES

To confuse things further, but not in this book, some plants have acquired a trade name. This appears after the Latin name, in a different typeface, and has no inverted commas. It is then followed by a name that may make no sense. These are given to plants where Plant Varietal Rights (PVR) apply, and where, if you were to propagate it for re-selling, a patent fee would apply. I make no apologies for not including these names. They are a selling tool that only serves to bewilder the average gardener. But be aware that if you intend to propagate perennials commercially, especially new varieties, it's a good idea to search the internet to check whether they have been registered with a PVR.

This is *Geranium* 'Gerwat'. We know it by its familiar trade name, 'Rozanne'

ABOUT PERENNIALS

The flowers of perennials come in many shapes and sizes, reflecting the different ways the plants create seed to reproduce. Before they can do this, the flowers have to encourage a wide range of pollinating insects to transfer pollen onto the reproductive organs of the flower. Their reward is nutritious, sugar-rich nectar.

The flower shape can affect which insects visit: upward-facing daisies and saucer-shaped flowers, for example, provide a stable platform for butterflies (which cannot enter bell-shaped flowers) as well as smaller bees.

Large bumblebees, because of their weight, need bigger flowers, such as peonies.

The number of flowers a plant produces each year can also affect how long it lives. *Catananche* and *Centranthus* both produce lots of flowers, but neither is long-lived. However, they do provide masses of seeds as an insurance policy. Plants with big flowers that produce only a few seeds, such as peonies and irises, live for a long time. This may be because their natural habitat is harsh so they need to reserve energy for survival, and not put it into seed production.

FLOWER SHAPES AND FORMS

Petals come in various arrangements and numbers. These are the forms referred to in this book:

- **Single** flowers have one row of petals
- **Semi-double** flowers have two, perhaps three, rows of petals
- **Double** flowers have lots of petals
- **Bell-shaped** flowers are long or cupped, and can hang down or face upwards
- **Trumpet-shaped** flowers are long and thin, the petals splaying outwards at the end
- **Tubular** flowers are long and thin. They are often carried thickly up flower stems to form a 'poker'
- **Clusters** and **sprays** sit towards the end of the flower stems
- **Heads** and **umbels** are carried at the top of the stem, where several flowers with short stalks grow outwards from a single point
- **Spikes** and **spires** are formed by a series of stalkless flowers carried up a single stem

LEAVES, COLOUR, SHAPE, TEXTURE

The shape of leaves, like that of the flowers, also varies greatly. They can be upright, long, and thin; oval or pointed; big or small. Some have serrated edges, others are crinkled or pleated. Smaller leaves are often carried along leaf stems to form a larger leaf, known as pinnate (like a feather), while bigger leaves are usually carried individually.

The leaves of most perennials are green, but the shade can vary from soft to dark. Some are grey, green-blue or yellow, while others look red, purple, or brown; and a few plants have almost black leaves. Variegated leaves come in more than one colour, the green broken with white or cream. The surface of a leaf often tells us where the plant grows naturally. Those with soft, furry, or velvety leaves may come from very dry locations. Really shiny leaves are often more or less evergreen, and are adapted to low light in shady positions.

The stiff, lacy ruff (bracts) of *Eryngium alpinum* protects the flower

Bell-shaped flowers of *Campanula* 'Iridescent Bells'

BOTANICAL TERMS USED

- **BRACTS** are found right at the base of the flower and can look rather like leaves
- **CALYX** is the collective name for the sepals, which wrap around the flower when it is in bud. They are usually green and when the flower is open, they sit at the base
- **STAMENS** are found in the centre of the flower and carry the all-important pollen needed for reproduction

Leaves of *Bergenia* and *Pulmonaria*

The most effective borders look like they are rising naturally from the soil, with plants that vary in heights and spreads. It doesn't matter if the border is seen from one side or all sides; every plant is part of the whole patchwork. Some perennials will naturally stand out – usually the tallest and boldest – and one plant will shine for a while before retreating to allow another to carry on the performance. For a successful border, choose plants that not only grow to different heights, but that also flower for long periods. And perennials combine perfectly with shrubs, annuals, and bulbs, (*see* p. 29), which add structure or fill gaps in different seasons of the year.

When it comes to selecting plants, we are all tempted by a pretty picture. But is it the right plant? There seem to be so many to choose from. Our nursery alone grows over 1000 different perennials. The easiest way might be to simplify the choice and limit the numbers, concentrating on irises, grasses, or perhaps white-flowered plants. That is one option, but given the wealth of perennials out there, why not make a border zing with colour and texture from spring to autumn?

So where do you start? Firstly, don't worry if you put a plant in the wrong place; I've often done this myself. Almost all perennials can be moved at any time as long as the top growth is cut back (to limit the plant's need for water). Secondly, remember that plants need to grow in the right place, so always check the soil type and how much light there is. It's no use putting a beautiful *Trillium* that needs humus-rich ground in dry, sandy soil. It just won't grow.

(*see* p. 29)

CONSIDERING THE CHOICE

Having decided to grow perennials, the next step is to choose them. For experienced or keen gardeners, this can be a great source of joy; for anyone new to gardening, the sheer choice of plants can be daunting. Below are a few helpful guidelines:

The main things to consider

- What soil type or types do you have in your garden? Be aware that soil in one area may be different to that in other areas
- How much light will the plants get?
- How tall do you want the plants to grow?
- How wide (the spread) do you want them to be?
- When do you want them to flower?
- Which flower colours do you like?

Other things to consider

- How long do you want a plant to stay in flower. Does it matter if the period is fairly short?
- Is it an easy plant to grow?
- Has it got an AGM (*see* p. 35)?
- Do the flowers attract insects?
- Can the flowers be cut for the house?
- How hardy is the plant?

(*see* p. 35)

A partially shaded border in July

This border is in shade for most of the day

When I plant up a new garden the first thing I look at is the soil. It is one of the most important elements in the garden, both feeding and watering the plants and so providing them with the energy to grow and thrive. While most perennials grow in any well-drained soil, certain soils can present more of a challenge. If you think your soil falls into this category, it's important to check first to make sure. You can easily tell what sort of soil you have by just grabbing a handful and examining it.

TYPES OF SOIL

Soil is divided into different types and all of them have features that affect the amount of moisture and nutrients available to a plant. A garden often contains a range of soils. Some areas may contain clay; in other parts, the soil may be very dry. This is especially true of new gardens where rubble lies beneath the soil. It is important to remember that no two gardens are alike. These are the most common soil types:

Loam soils

Loam soils are the best of all. They are dark in colour and when rubbed between the fingers crumble easily. They drain well, but do not dry out, which means they are rich in nutrients. They are also easy to dig. Almost all plants will grow in this soil.

Clay soils

Pale and sticky to the touch, clay soils do not drain easily, and are often lumpy, which can make them difficult to dig. Some clay soils are rich in loam. These drain more freely, but still hold water for a long time. Clay and clay-loam mixes are rich in nutrients. These plants happily grow in clay soils:

Aconitum	Helenium
Actaea	Hosta
Aster	Inula
Astrantia	Kirengeshoma
Astilbe	Ligularia
Brunnera	Monarda
Cirsium	Persicaria
Epimedium	Prunella
Eupatorium	Pulmonaria
Geranium	Rudbeckia

Chalk soils

Containing lots of white chalk or flint pieces, these soils are usually pale in colour, are almost always alkaline (*see* right) and often shallow. They are very free-draining so nutrients are quickly washed out. The plants below cope with chalky, alkaline soils:

Achillea	Phlomis
Bergenia	Salvia
Campanula	Sedum
Dianthus	Sidalcea
Eryngium	Verbascum
Euphorbia	Verbena
Origanum	

Sandy soils

Sandy soils can be brown or red. They are made up of small particles that, when dry, run easily through the fingers. This type of soil is very free draining, so nutrients are quickly leached out, rendering the soil poor. Plants suitable for sandy soils are listed below:

Acanthus	Linaria
Achillea	Lychnis coronaria
Centhranthus	Oenothera
Echinops	Origanum
Eryngium	Salvia
Iris, bearded types	Saxifraga
Knautia	Valeriana
Lamium	Verbascum

Silver-leaved plants thrive in a dry border

Iris pseudacorus growing in damp soil in partial shade

DRAINAGE and ACID/ALKALINE SOILS

The majority of plants described in this book will grow in good, well-drained soils. Such soils drain reasonably quickly even after heavy rain, and they contain ample nutrients and a balanced pH. The pH of a soil refers to how acid or alkaline it is. There are very few perennials that require only an acid or alkaline soil. But certain perennials fare better in acid soils than others and these generally grow in soil that remains moist (*see* below). Those that will not thrive in acid soil include bearded irises and *Dianthus*. For perennials that prefer alkaline soils, which contain lots of chalk or flint, *see* Chalk soils, below left.

Wet soils

These are soils that remain wet or moist even during hot summers. They are most likely to be found around or near ponds and streams, and include boggy areas. The plants below thrive in wet soils in sun or partial shade:

Astilbe	Ligularia
Hosta	Lobelia
Iris ensata	Lysimachia
Iris laevigata	Lythrum
Iris pseudacorus	Primula
Iris sibirica	Rodgersia

Dry soils

A dry soil is most definitely a disadvantage when growing perennials. These soils, which include chalky and sandy soils, are often poor in nutrients. During hot spells they become so dry the plants suffer. Dry soil can also be found beneath trees and shrubs, along the edges of stone and brick walls, and on sloping banks. These plants will tolerate dry soils:

Asphodeline	Erodium
Calamintha	Eryngium
Campanula	Gypsophila
Coreopsis	Iris, bearded types
Dianthus	Sedum
Dictamnus	Stachys byzantina
Echinops	Stipa

The amount of light a garden receives determines which plants will flourish. While many gardens have areas that get lots of sun for most of the day, there will always be spots where the light is limited. To find the aspect of your garden, notice where the sun rises (east) and work round from there. South-facing gardens are always the sunniest and warmest. West, however, is often the best, as gardens with this aspect receive an even amount of light and shade. North-facing gardens can be difficult for plants, especially if the soil is dry, whereas easterly borders can be the coolest. Fortunately, perennials are a diverse group: some thrive in light shade, very few grow with very little sunlight. Most of the plants in this book will flourish in a sunny position or one that is in shade for part of the day.

HOW MUCH SUN?

The sections below give some guidance on how to judge the amount of sun in your garden. This will vary according to the time of day, or season, and also if the garden is overshadowed by buildings or trees. The sun, of course, is at its highest in summer and at its lowest in winter, when few herbaceous perennials are growing.

Full sun

A site with full sun receives light throughout the day. If the soil is poor, it will dry out quickly, which some plants resent.

Partial shade

These sites get some sunlight for a good proportion of the day, for example from 10am to 4pm. Areas under the eaves of a house and along the margins of tall trees and shrubs will be partially shaded.

Shade

Full shade does limit a gardener's choices yet there is still a wide range of plants on offer, many of which are spring-flowering. The plants below will grow in a shady spot in soil that does not dry out entirely. Those that will tolerate dry soils have an asterisk*.

Actaea | Linaria
Aquilegia | Liriope
Aruncus | Lunaria
Astilbe | Meconopsis
Astrantia | Melittis
Bergenia | Omphalodes
Brunnera | Persicaria
Campanula latifolia* | Polygonatum*
Dicentra | Primula
Epimedium | Pulmonaria
Euphorbia (some)* | Symphytum
Geranium (some)* | Tellima*
Helleborus | Trillium
Hosta | Tricyrtis
Iris foetidissima* | Uvularia
Kirengeshoma | Viola
Lamium | Waldsteinia
Lamprocapnos

The clay-loam soil drains well in this sunny border because it slopes

HILLSIDE GARDENS

Our garden is relatively low-lying at 300 feet (100 metres) above sea level, compared to plots on the side of hills or mountains. Yet we still get a lot of rain and it can be windy. The obvious plants to grow are those that tolerate wet soil (see p. 11) and short plants. However, a few tall varieties with slender stems that bend with the wind cope well. These include *Sanguisorba* and *Valeriana*.

COASTAL GARDENS

Having never gardened down by the sea, I have consulted other specialists' lists of plants that will grow in a salty position. These are their suggestions:

Achillea | Kniphofia
Anemone | Lathyrus
Anthemis | Limonium
Asters, short types | Linaria
Campanula | Mertensia
Catananche | Morina
Centranthus | Oenothera
Crocosmia | Origanum
Dianthus | Penstemon
Echinops | Physostegia
Erigeron | Potentilla
Eryngium | Salvia
Euphorbia | Scabiosa
Geranium | Sedum
Hesperantha | Stachys
Heuchera | Stokesia
Iris | Veronica

HARDINESS

As perennials come back year after year, by definition they are hardy. But there are limits to their hardiness. Most of the plants described in this book will survive a temperature down to -15°C, or lower. In 2010 the temperature dipped to -19.5°C at our nursery in mid-Shropshire, yet the vast majority of the plants were fine. However, a few perennials will suffer if the temperature drops below -5°C, especially if the ground is wet. These include *Penstemon* and *Verbena*.

This border gets sunlight for just a few hours a day, yet the right choice of plants ensures a good range of colour

While *Verbena bonariensis* copes well with high winds, it can suffer in cold winters

I build up my beds and borders in layers, creating the picture as I go, working from front to back. What I am aiming for is a kind of rhythm, which will be created by plants that differ in height, colour, and flowering time. However, knowing where to start can be difficult – like being faced with a blank piece of paper at an exam.

If I am undertaking a big project, such as a whole new border, I plan the scheme out on a piece of paper, drawing a circle for each plant variety. This stops me from repeating plants and making the border too regimented. I tend to group each variety together, and then 'drift' the groups across the soil, making irregular, overlapping shapes and avoiding straight lines. Designers advise us to plant in groups of three, but as long as you grow sufficient key varieties in large numbers, less-critical varieties can be added in ones or twos. These will balance the border by filling the space between the larger groups and stop it from looking 'blocky.' The mainstays of the scheme are the plants that flower the longest and provide the most structure, such as hardy geraniums, *Salvia*, *Nepeta*, and *Campanula*.

Yet, however carefully you prepare, things may not go strictly according to plan. In the process of choosing plants, some may not be available, while others not on the list catch your eye. This is the beauty of gardening – like nature, it needs to evolve organically.

Timmy the cat enjoying the evening sun

The lawns of the front garden are enclosed by narrow borders. Soft mounds of *Geranium* 'Blue Cloud', *Geum* 'Pink Frills', and *Campanula glomerata* 'Caroline' break up the straight lines

A layered effect created with *Gillenia trifoliata* (front), *Salvia nemorosa* 'Amethyst', and *Astrantia major* (back)

Planted on a corner, *Paeonia* 'Cora Louise' makes a statement

When choosing what to grow along the front of the border, consider what is at its edge. Many of my borders have grass paths alongside and, because plants spread and I am not disciplined enough to cut them back, the grass at the edge tends to die off. Fortunately, it regrows.

The most useful plants for the front, even if you do have grass alongside, are those that spread. They soften harsh lines created by paving slabs, bricks, and timber, and they can be tucked in neatly in front of taller plants, leaving no bare earth. But spreading plants with spreading roots may turn into thugs that rapidly invade their surroundings. The solution, strange though it may seem, is to grow two thugs together. *Stachys byzantina* will romp away, but a good companion like *Persicaria affinis* will keep it in check. There are also neater plants for the front of a border such as *Bergenia* and *Geum*. Slow-growing, they are easily controlled if they get too big.

I don't always use short plants for the front of a border, despite convention. Taller plants, provided they have slender flower stems, can also be grown at the front. They create a transparent 'screen' that allows you to look through to plants growing behind.

LOW, SPREADING PLANTS

Plants marked with an asterisk can be thugs
*Ajuga**
Alchemilla mollis
Bergenia
Campanula glomerata and *punctata* types
Epimedium
Geranium 'Mavis Simpson'
Geranium 'Rozanne'
Geranium × riversleaianum 'Russell Prichard'
Geranium sanguineum types
Geum
Lamium
Origanum
*Persicaria affinis**
Potentilla
Prunella
Sanguisorba officinalis 'Red Thunder'
Saxifraga × urbium
*Stachys byzantina**
Veronica
Waldsteinia

Sanguisorba 'Pink Tanna' is quite tall, yet creates a lovely 'see-through' effect

Running along the north-facing side of the house, loose clumps of magenta *Geranium psilostemon* and lime-green *Alchemilla mollis* soften the geometry of the path

Having chosen the plants for the front or edges of the border, it's time to fill in the rest of the picture. The plants that form the bulk of your scheme will sit in the middle layer, providing the colours and shapes that will knit the border together. I rarely select plants of similar heights and shapes because this leads to a rigid, uninteresting border that lacks contrast.

Mixing plants with different forms and foliage, this May-blooming group of *Paeonia* 'Picotee' (back), *Stachys byzantina* 'Big Ears', and *Centaurea montana* 'Carnea' (front) will be interesting even after the flowers have faded

The flowers of *Geum* 'Mai Tai' are carried on tall stems that erupt from a mound of leaves

Aster 'Wood's Pink' mixes happily with low-growing *Origanum laevigatum* 'Herrenhausen'

MOUNDING PLANTS

Good for padding, plants that form domed mounds often have small flowers which, from a distance, look like a mass of dots scattered over the leaves. Some carry the flowers in sprays on long stems and create a shape that can be wider than it is high. The leaves of mounding plants are also useful in that they often smother the ground and prevent weeds from emerging. Place them together and mounding plants will compete for room, but unless one is much smaller than the other, each will find its own space.

There are many examples of mounding plants – far too many to list. Those I consider indispensable and have included in all my gardens are:

Aster	*Geum*
Centaurea	*Nepeta*
Geranium	*Salvia*

UPRIGHT CLUMPING PLANTS

While mounding plants fill space from the ground upwards, upright plants create structure. The straight stems are often rigid, and topped with flowers that are held high enough to be seen over other plants. The flowers of tall plants are, I hesitate to say, perhaps more important than the leaves, although the early leaves will add to spring's varied green tapestry. If the plant is set further back in a border, its leaves are often hidden by the time the flowers arrive.

It is important to consider how the flowers are carried on upright plants as this affects the amount of colour on display. Perennials with long spikes of flowers (*Nepeta*) and clusters (*Helenium*) are great for solid colour. If the flower stems carry fewer flowers, the effect is wispy. Perennials with big flowers carried at well-spaced intervals, on the other hand, add accents of colour. A lot of foliage will be visible with these plants so try to arrange them in the border by leaf shape rather than flower colour.

All these plants have upright, straight, leafy stems that emerge from a central crown:

Achillea	*Eupatorium*
Agastache	*Gillenia*
Anemone	*Geum*
Aster	*Helenium*
Astrantia	*Lychnis*
Campanula	*Lysimachia*
Centranthus	*Monarda*
Echinacea	*Phlox*
Echinops	*Thalictrum*

Plants in this grouping have different yet complementary habits, flower forms, and colours. From the front: *Achillea* 'Forncett Fletton', *Stemmacantha centaureoides* with *Persicaria affinis*, *Lychnis coronaria*, and *Salvia nemorosa* 'Amethyst, then *Nepeta* 'Six Hills Giant'

Tall, erect plants add height and interest to a dark background. *Eupatorium purpureum* and *Veronicastrum virginicum* 'Fascination' rise behind *Persicaria amplexicaulis* 'Taurus' and burnt-orange *Helenium* 'Moerheim Beauty'

TALL PERENNIALS

The back of the border is usually reserved for tall, dominant plants. However, some of my borders are surrounded by paths, so I grow tall varieties in the middle where they can be seen from all sides.

Wherever you want to grow the tallest plants, make sure they have strong, rigid stems and won't topple over on to lower-growing plants. Some are very graceful, carrying their blooms in slender spikes on slim flower stems. These create a 'see-through' effect. Others, such as *Eupatorium*, have dome-shaped flowers and leafy stems, which encourage the eye to drift upwards. Delphiniums and verbascums, on the other hand, carry the flowers down the stems, arresting the gaze and acting rather like a punctuation mark.

UPRIGHT SPIRES

Plants with an asterisk are 'see-through'

Aconitum	*Valeriana**
Delphinium	*Verbascum**
*Linaria**	*Verbena**
Persicaria	*Veronica**
Stipa	*Veronicastrum**

FOCAL POINTS

Plants used as focal points don't have to be big, they just have to stand out from the crowd. A dark background can also be used to highlight a particular plant. I have a shady area next to a small copse where white campanulas really shine (*see* below, left).

It is, however, height or colour that tends to draw the eye. In early summer, colourful irises and peonies – both plants with big flowers – make good focal points. By midsummer, elegant *Thalictrum* towers above its neighbours, while in autumn massive *Eupatorium* takes centre stage, as do tall grasses.

Whatever you grow, only grow one of a kind. I have two varieties of *Thalictrum* that swamp each other, making it difficult to focus on either of these glorious plants. Irises can clash if you aren't careful with colour, so the effect is lost. Be restrained; less is often more.

These are just some of the plants I have used as focal points:

Aconitum	*Persicaria*
Aruncus	*Phlox*
Eupatorium	*Stipa gigantea*
Iris	*Thalictrum*
Paeonia	

Stipa gigantea is a bold, dignified addition to the back of a border

Campanula persicifolia var. *alba* stands out against a shady background

Flowering is just one stage in the growing process of a plant. We grow perennials for their beautiful flowers, but they can also look fabulous from the first moment their young foliage pokes out of the ground to their final flourish in autumn. It pays to consider all stages in the plant's growth cycle when deciding which perennials to plant.

LEAF SHOOTS

The early shoots of some perennials are beautifully shaped, while others send up red-tinged new foliage. Both add to the delight of spring growth. Try these:

Dicentra
Euphorbia
Gillenia
Hosta
Lathyrus
Paeonia
Rhodiola
Sedum
Veronicastrum

FLOWER BUDS

Buds, like flowers, can be distinctive and sculptural. The plants listed below have eye-catching buds, and those marked with an asterisk also have lovely stems.

Eryngium
Iris*
Kniphofia
Lysimachia
 clethroides*
Meconopsis
Oenothera*
Papaver
Paeonia*
Sanguisorba

SEEDHEADS

Once the flowers have gone to seed, the heads of many perennials create great structure and provide wildlife with winter food. These plants have lasting seedheads:

Achillea
Anemone
Astrantia
Dictamnus
Echinops
Eryngium
Iris
Lunaria
Meconopsis
Papaver
Sedum
Selinum

Early shoots of *Veronicastrum*

Iris × robusta 'Gerald Darby' in bud

Some heads of *Selinum wallichianum* turn to seed as others open

Phlox paniculata 'Amethyst' is both a focal point and scented

Fragrant *Paeonia* 'Auguste Dessert' with *Salvia nemorosa* 'Amethyst'

FRAGRANT FLOWERS

Scent is an important attribute and one that many gardeners look for in a plant. Most perennial flowers have none or very little, but there are some exceptions. Certain varieties of *Phlox*, *Paeonia*, and *Dianthus*, for example, do emit a delicious scent. Even then, the fragrance is sometimes obvious only when the weather is warm or the flowers are cut and brought into a warm room. Check the plant descriptions for fragrance and also consider the following groups, which have scented varieties:

Actaea
Dianthus
Echinacea
Hemerocallis (yellow
varieties)
Iris
Paeonia
Phlox
Primula
Valeriana

Daisy-shaped *Echinacea purpurea* 'Hope'

Starry flowers of *Aster laterifolius* 'Prince'

Campanula punctata f. *rubriflora* has bell-shaped flowers

Flower spikes of *Verbascum chaixii* 'Album'

Primulas have saucer-shaped flowers

Big flowers of tall bearded *Iris* 'New Leaf'

Size and shape are important considerations when choosing plants, but it is what the flower looks like that is top of most people's list. To create an interesting border, it's vital to put flowers of varying shapes together.

DAISIES AND STARS

The most abundant flower form is the daisy or star shape. Smaller flowers, such as those of *Calamintha* are often produced in large numbers, creating fluffy sprays. Bigger daisy flowers, like *Echinacea*, have larger petals and are especially colourful. The flowers of some plants consist of many small daisies that open into tightly knitted, flat heads, like *Achillea*. Taking the eye across, rather than up, they mix well with other shapes.

BELLS

Perennials with bell-shaped flowers, like *Campanula*, are often demure, whatever their size. These don't shout colour from the rooftops, but sit very comfortably among their more brightly coloured neighbours.

SPIKES

Plants that carry the flowers the length of the flower stems, such as *Verbascum* and *Persicaria*, create a vertical exclamation mark, which complements and contrasts with all other flower shapes. The poker-shaped flowers of *Kniphofia* have the same effect, but the colour is limited to the top of the flower stem.

SAUCERS

Many perennials have flat, saucer-shaped flowers. Often small, some, like *Phlox*, open into tight, colourful heads, while in others, such as *Geranium*, the flowers are more randomly scattered, producing a less colourful, but more textural plant.

BIG FLOWERS

The largest flowers, with the biggest petals, are usually the most colourful. Peonies and irises have generous-sized flowers that come in an amazing range of vibrant as well as gentle tones. While these may be dramatic, blending them with other plants isn't easy because their flowers can easily overpower more delicate ones. The best option is to grow these not in clumps, but as individuals, choosing varieties that will flower before neighbouring border plants begin to bloom.

Contrasting flower shapes create foreground interest – and colour – without blocking the glorious view. From left to right: *Phlox paniculata* 'Eva Cullum', *Persicaria amplexicaulis* 'Taurus', *Verbascum chaixii* 'Album', and *Helenium* 'Sahin's Early Flowerer'

Colour for me is one of the most important attributes of a flower but I'm not precious about how colours are combined in a border. Most sit happily together, with one exception: I find really vivid pink – the shade of fuchsia- or lipstick-pink – next to bright orange very uncomfortable. However, if the orange plant is placed at a distance from the pink one, the two colours don't fight. Combining colours is a matter of individual taste, so I don't want to be prescriptive. However, when spending money on plants, some gardeners want to be confident that their choices aren't going to clash horribly. If you are unsure, choose plants by colour and tone: rich, strong colours work well together, or opt for soft shades. Selecting just one colour is another option – white being the most common choice.

SOFT COLOURS

The easiest perennials to combine in terms of colour are those with soft pastel flowers. And there are many. Shades of pearly pink, powder-blue, and pure white abound in a variety of flower shapes and forms. You'll never be stuck for a tall, pale-pink, spiky plant, or a low, spreading one. Softly coloured plants are easy on the eye, but they can lack sparkle. Add rich blue, perhaps a hardy geranium or *Salvia*, and the whole scheme will be lifted. To bring the best out of these colours, go further and add soft-yellow flowers, for example *Coreopsis verticillata* 'Moonbeam'.

HOT COLOURS

Perennials with brightly coloured flowers are relatively few in number. Vivid red, rich orange, or sunshine-yellow are not as common in perennials' wild ancestors (from which our garden varieties are bred) as softer shades. Late-summer and early autumn borders with really hot, intense colour are difficult to achieve without incorporating tender cannas and dahlias, but perennials such as *Paeonia*, *Iris*, *Hemerocallis*, and *Phlox* do offer rich colour and will add a dash of boldness. But be restrained – too many big flowers in strong shades can be jarring. Those with smaller, yet vibrant flowers are useful for blending in smaller groups. I love orange *Geum* with dark purple *Salvia*, and rich-lilac *Aster* with yellow *Rudbeckia*.

Geranium 'Dragon Heart' with *Salvia nemorosa* 'Ostfriesland'

Achillea 'Pretty Belinda', *Sanguisorba menziesii*, and *Centaurea montana* 'Carnea'

Phlox paniculata 'White Admiral' with *Persicaria amplexicaulis* 'Taurus'

Rudbeckia trifoliata with *Aster novae-angliae* 'Mrs S. T. Wright'

Centranthus ruber with *Geranium* 'Brookside'

Helenium 'Wyndley' with *Nepeta* × *faassenii* 'Kit Cat'

COLOUR FOR PLANTAHOLICS

I have no discipline when it comes to plants and being a plant collector can be a curse when designing a garden. I can't restrict the variety of plants I grow, or plant them in garden designer-type drifts of threes or fives. I plant perennials in ones or twos otherwise I would need acres, which would be unmanageable. My solution, which also avoids too many colour clashes, is twofold. Firstly, I graduate colours, so blocks of pastel colours merge gradually with flowers of darker tones. Secondly, I grow different plants with similar-coloured flowers near to each other, such as *Nepeta* 'Six Hills Giant' with *Geranium* 'Orion'. This means I don't have to restrict the number of plants I grow.

LIMITING COLOURS

At the beginning of the last century, Vita Sackville-West successfully created a white garden at Sissinghurst Castle in Kent. It is described as white, but it is really a white and green garden. Unless planted in large numbers, I rarely include white-flowered perennials in a border as they can be dominant, although the colour is good in a dark spot. Using only one colour, perhaps blue or pink, would not only limit the choice of plants, it could also look and feel bland. One option is to go for two different flower colours: pink and blue; white and yellow; or red and purple. These combinations, though rather restricting in terms of plant varieties, can be quite stunning.

The mauve-blue of *Centaurea* 'Blewitt' picks up the red tones of *Astrantia major* 'Claret' in this eye-catching pairing

The pale tones of *Astrantia major* and *Veronicastrum virginicum* 'Pink Glow' work well in this planting of soft colours

Whether you are creating a border or just grouping a few new plants together, the foliage will be on show well before and after the flowers. Put plants with the same colour and similar shapes of leaf next to one another and the picture will have no definition, and may even be dull. But combine different leaf colours, shapes, and textures, and you will create a fabulous patchwork with shades of green, brown, silver, and yellow throughout the year.

COLOURED LEAVES

The main colour of leaves is, naturally, green, but look more closely and you will notice different tones varying from light to dark, as well as effects created by the leaf texture. Glossy leaves reflect light and define the three-dimensional quality of the plant, while hairs on leaves flatten the surface colour. Those leaves that invite you to touch them are often silver, for example furry *Stachys byzantina*. Silver foliage will also brighten up a dark spot, as does yellow, although it's best to avoid certain yellow-leaved plants, such as blue-flowered *Centaurea montana* 'Gold Bullion'. Its flowers and leaves clash badly and can look garish.

Very dark and-near black leaves are some of the most handsome. They are invaluable for adding contrast to a border, and they give definition to plants as well as flowers.

VARIEGATED LEAVES

The presence of two colours on the leaves is invariably the result of a lack of chlorophyll. This weakens the surface of the leaf, so variegated plants may need to be grown in partial shade to prevent sun damage. The splashes and patches of white or pale cream are not to everyone's taste, but I use plants with variegated foliage to add extra colour and to knit certain colours together, such as green and purple.

SCENTED LEAVES

Leaves of perennials can be scented, but it is often only apparent when the leaf is rubbed or crushed between the fingers or when brushed against. Roots can also be fragrant (peony roots have a very strong aroma, as do some irises) but you only discover this when dividing a plant. The following have scented foliage:

Agastache	*Nepeta*
Calamintha	*Origanum*
Geranium	*Salvia*
macrorrhizum	*Valeriana*
Monarda	

LEAVES THAT CHANGE COLOUR

Unless they are evergreen, leaves don't stay the same all year: autumn hits most of them eventually. Some morph early in the season, such as the variegated leaves of *Astrantia major* 'Sunningdale Variegated', which turn plain green as the flowers open.

While autumn is the classic time for fiery colour in shrubs and trees, most perennials quickly disintegrate into a mass of brown leaves and stems when the temperature drops below 10°C. Some, like *Gillenia trifoliata*, remain handsome for a few weeks, but if you want year-round foliage colour, try bergenias. From autumn to spring, the leaves are burnished with red and purple.

PERENNIALS WITH HANDSOME LEAVES

The perennials listed below are just some of the varieties with distinctive foliage.

Actaea D	*Hakonechloa* V
Ajuga E	*Heuchera* D
Anaphalis S	*Hosta* V, Y
Astrantia (some) E	*Lysimachia* D
Bergenia E	*Milium* Y
Brunnera types S, V	*Miscanthus* V
Calamagrostis V	*Ophiopogon* D
Campanula E	*Pulmonaria* S
Dianthus S	*Sedum* D, Y
Epimedium E	*Stachys* S
Eryngium V	*Thalictrum* Y
Euphorbia E	*Valeriana* Y
Geranium (some) E	*Waldsteinia* D

Key D dark leaves, E evergreen, S silver, V variegated, Y yellow

Autumn foliage of *Gillenia trifoliata*

Sedum telephium 'Xenox' behind
Stachys byzantina 'Big Ears'

Variegated *Lysimachia punctata* 'Alexander'

Before selecting your perennials, it's important to consider when a plant will be in flower. A garden that flowers just for a month or two is a missed opportunity, but an easy trap to fall into. We are inclined to buy plants because we want colour when the garden is most used. Yet it is possible to have perennials in flower each month of the year. This might take a little planning, and you may need slightly more space, but it is not difficult to achieve. Sometimes it is easier to divide parts of the garden, or a big border, into the two main seasons: spring and summer. Planting small groups of perennials that flower at the same time of year together, rather than spreading them thinly, gives a sense of cohesion.

SPANNING THE SEASONS

One part of my garden is designed to be in full flower during July and August, a time when the majority of perennials bloom. It is also when the sun is at its highest, and the days are at their longest and warmest. This part of the garden is where we sit in the evenings, sipping a glass of wine, watching the sun go down. However, even when these borders are not in full bloom, they look interesting. In spring they are a tapestry of green, with leaves of all shapes, sizes, and colours merging, quickly covering the ground to prevent weeds. The first perennials start to bloom in May. These are mainly *Geum* and *Centaurea*. In June the bold flowers of irises and peonies catch the eye, and by high summer *Phlox*, *Achillea*, *Veronicastrum*, *Nepeta*, and *Persicaria* create a riot of colour. Some plants fade as the days shorten, but asters and anemones continue, sometimes as late as November and hellebore flowers add winter interest (*see* p. 26 Essential Perennials By Month).

May

July

June

September

A spring display of *Geranium sylvaticum* 'Album', sky-blue *Brunnera macrophylla* 'Blaukuppel', and *Lamprocapnos spectabilis*

SPRING PLANTS

Other parts of my garden are dedicated to spring-flowering plants. These generally bloom beneath trees or shrubs, the plants retreating as the canopy of leaves fills out. Others, such as early dwarf irises and *Pulmonaria* are planted near to the house where I can enjoy them. In the early part of the year I spend more time gazing out of windows, wishing for warm weather, than I do in the garden.

AUTUMN AND WINTER PLANTS

Autumn-blooming plants grow happily with the plants that are the mainstays of the summer border. They are fewer in number so don't need a separate area. The range of perennials that flower in winter is also limited, but interest is provided by plants with evergreen foliage, and hellebore flowers are always a welcome sight.

ESSENTIAL PERENNIALS BY MONTH

If you aim to maintain year-round interest, choose a plant from each month and your garden should have something in flower in all four seasons. These are the main groups of perennials I use and find reliable in the garden. But remember that a plant might start to bloom one month and still be in flower some months later. Flowering times do overlap and, depending on where you live, plants may bloom earlier or later.

FEBRUARY

Pulmonaria	

MARCH

Bergenia	*Pulmonaria*
Lathyrus	

APRIL

Brunnera	*Lamprocapnos*
Epimedium	*Primula*

MAY

Aquilegia	*Geum*
Astrantia	*Lupin*
Campanula	*Papaver*
Centaurea	*Veronica*
Geranium	

JUNE

Alchemilla	*Iris*
Astrantia	*Knautia*
Campanula	*Paeonia*
Cirsium	*Salvia*
Geranium	*Verbena*

JULY

Achillea	*Monarda*
Echinops	*Nepeta*
Erigeron	*Persicaria*
Eryngium	*Phlox*
Gillenia	*Potentilla*
Hemerocallis	*Sanguisorba*
Leucanthemum	*Thalictrum*
Lychnis	*Tradescantia*
Lysimachia	

AUGUST

Aconitum	*Eupatorium*
Anemone	*Helenium*
Calamintha	*Kniphofia*
Coreopsis	*Rudbeckia*
Crocosmia	*Veronicastrum*
Echinacea	

SEPTEMBER

Actaea	*Sedum*
Aster	

OCTOBER

Chrysanthemum	*Tricyrtis*

NOVEMBER, DECEMBER, JANUARY

Helleborus	

September border with (back to front) tall *Eupatorium maculatum* 'Riesenschirm', *Helenium*, *Monarda* 'Prärienacht', *Sedum telephium* 'Purple Emperor' and white *Echinacea*

Butterflies and bees are important plant pollinators and their contribution to the garden cannot be underestimated, especially if you grow fruit or vegetables. These small creatures also bring welcome sound and movement to the border. In the UK there are over 250 different types of bees and bumblebees and around 60 different butterflies, plus many more moths, a few of them flying during the day. In my garden it is easy to spot at least seven species of butterflies at any one time, as well as a dozen different bees. Other creatures, such as birds and hedgehogs, also deter pests.

Nectar-rich flowers

To encourage insects into your garden, it is important to grow a wide variety of plants in different parts of your plot. Butterflies and bees are generally attracted to simply shaped, single flowers, like daisies, because the composition allows nectar to be accessed easily. Unlike delicate butterflies and honeybees, which don't touch down to feed for long, big-bodied bumblebees need sturdy flowers to carry their weight.

Other flying creatures

In addition to bees and butterflies, there are many other beneficial insects that you can encourage. The adults and larvae of ladybirds and lacewings eat aphids, as well as other small insects, helping to control unwanted pests. Hoverflies, easily mistaken for bees, are also great pollinators. Sometimes small black beetles, called pollen beetles, can be seen digging into yellow flowers and may help with pollination. The much-feared wasp also loves nectar, and the young of some types will feed on insects.

BIRDS AND SMALL ANIMALS

When a garden is full of flowers, insects will appear, quickly followed by birds, attracted first by the wealth of edible insect life, and later by nutritious seedheads. Frogs, toads, and even hedgehogs are also likely to skulk beneath plants, seeking out succulent slugs, snails, and other delights.

ESSENTIAL BEE- AND BUTTERFLY-ATTRACTING PERENNIALS

Aster	Nepeta
Centaurea	Origanum
Echinacea	Persicaria
Echinops	Pulmonaria
Eupatorium	Sanguisorba
Helenium	Sedum
Monarda	Succisa
Lysimachia	

A bumblebee among stems of *Sanguisorba* 'Pink Tanna'

Eupatorium purpureum covered with large whites and a red admiral butterfly

A sparrow eating Japanese anemone seedheads left over winter

A baby hedgehog beneath *Aquilegia*

A comma butterfly on *Helenium*

A vase of peonies, *Achillea millefolium* 'Red Velvet', pale-pink *Astrantia* 'Buckland', blue *Centaurea*, *Veronica spicata*, and yellow-green *Alchemilla mollis*

PERENNIALS FOR POTS

Although many gardeners opt for brightly coloured annuals for containers, almost all perennials can be grown in this way. Chosen for their foliage interest, many perennials offer a subtle mix of textures and colours that blends easily into any setting. Perennials also need less feeding and watering, and are easier to maintain than many annual container plantings. Provided you choose a big pot, and provide a little food, a plant can be left for some years. I have, for example, grown hostas and *Hakonechloa* in the same containers for more than three years.

Perennials are a diverse bunch and certain plants are ideal for spots where annuals might not thrive. *Bergenia* and *Helleborus*, for example, are both happy in cool, shady areas, and their evergreen leaves create winter interest at a time when it is needed most. Hostas, too, like shade, and growing them in pots is often the best way to prevent marauding slugs from decimating the leaves. Conversely, really hot spots may not suit annuals. If the compost dries out, some annuals will die while certain perennials, such as *Dianthus*, and *Sedum*, can be revived with a good dowsing. Remember that most perennials are big plants so give each its own container. I do, however, tuck *Viola* and *Erigeron karvinskianus*, around the base of broader plants for extra colour.

Hakonechloa macra 'Aureola'

Hosta 'Patriot' in the shade

PERENNIALS FOR CUTTING

In years gone by, when all flowers for sale at markets were grown locally, perennials were essential to the trade. Today, when flowers are imported from all over the world, perennials are less popular, but there are many varieties that make beautiful cut flowers for the house.

Cottage-style cutting gardens

The easiest way to grow perennials for cutting, especially in smaller gardens, is in a border with other plants. The flowers of some (but not all) varieties can be removed without spoiling the appearance of the whole plant. The main drawback of this rather uncontrolled approach is that the flower stems may not be very straight or of a uniform size. If this isn't a major concern, plants for cutting can be successfully combined with others that you leave alone.

Formal cutting borders

In larger gardens, you can dedicate an area to growing flowers for cutting, in the same way as you would create a separate plot for vegetables. It's best to arrange the plants in neat rows for easy access. Tie in the flower stems as they grow upwards, as this will keep them perfectly straight. In this more functional area of the garden, appearance is not paramount so you can denude the mother plant by removing the flower stems. I simply use a pair of kitchen scissors to cut flowers from the garden, then immediately plunge the stems into water to seal the ends and prevent the flowers from wilting. The varieties in the list below will last from four to ten days in water.

CUT FLOWERS FOR THE HOUSE

An asterisk indicates a perennial plant best grown in a formal cutting garden or patch. Planted in a border, the plant would soon be denuded of flower and this would leave an unsightly gap.

*Achillea**	*Iris**
Alchemilla	*Knautia*
Aster	*Leucanthemum**
Astrantia	*Liatris**
Centaurea	*Paeonia**
Dianthus	*Persicaria*
*Echinacea**	*Phlox**
*Echinops**	*Sanguisorba*
*Eryngium**	*Scabiosa*
Geum	*Verbena**
Helenium	

Perennials are rarely grown in isolation. In the garden, they combine perfectly with annuals, bulbs, and, particularly, shrubs. Perennial plants will not only increase the richness and diversity of your garden, but they are indispensable for adding colour and form throughout the seasons.

Annuals

Growing and caring for annuals, which live for just one year, can be a labour intensive and expensive business. Yet they are useful for adding interest or for filling gaps while perennials mature. I have grown great swathes of white cosmos from seed to enliven a border of peonies that were no longer in flower. Sweet peas are another favourite, not just for the scent but for adding a vertical dimension. I grow them up metal obelisks in the middle of my square borders to create height and structure.

Bulbs

Spring, the time when bulbs are really at their best, is also the season when little else provides colour. In the north-facing border, near my kitchen, I planted little *Narcissus* 'Hiawatha' and elegant white-flowered *Narcissus* 'Thalia'. Both look particularly good with blue-flowered *Pulmonaria*. Under the shade of trees, low-growing *Epimedium* bears dainty flowers in spring, and next to giant *Thalictrum*, where I meant to plant *Lilium martagon*, I have another marvellous, tall lily, *Lilium* 'Lankon'. A happy mistake.

Shrubs

Apart from trees, there are no better plants than shrubs for year-round structure. Evergreen shrubs such as *Viburnum tinus* create a perfect backdrop for white-flowered perennials, such as anemone. Some of the best shrubs for growing with perennials are those with dark leaves – the rounded foliage of purple forms of *Cotinus* combines beautifully with iris blooms in shades of bronze or gold – while silver-leaved shrubs or shrubby *Potentilla* work really well nearer the front of a border.

The most obvious shrubs to grow with perennials are roses. Despite having a famous rose-grower for a father (David Austin), I currently have just two varieties in the garden. One bears my name, the other is *Rosa* 'James Galway' a plant with clusters of soft-pink, double, fragrant flowers that harmonise with mounds of *Geranium psilostemon*. In spring, this rose's fresh, dark-red foliage complements a nearby *Paeonia emodi* (Himalayan peony).

The heads of *Allium* 'Purple Sensation' add form and colour to this late-spring border

Sweet peas growing up a metal obelisk

Lilium 'Lankon' in a shady spot

The beautiful blooms of *Rosa* 'James Galway' mix perfectly with mounding perennials

Now for the practical aspects of creating a perennial garden. This is where the hard work begins, although for me this is the fun part where all the ideas and dreams for the garden finally get underway. Let's start with the plants. There are various ways of acquiring plants. When friends and relatives are splitting plants, you can beg a piece, promising something in return later. Some perennials can be grown from seed, others from cuttings, but most gardeners have to buy the plants that really catch their eye.

WHERE TO BUY PLANTS

For many, the first port of call is probably a garden centre. Most of them display plants only when looking their best and in full flower, which means the number of varieties in stock can be limited. Nurseries, whether small, large, retail, or mail order, are the answer. If you are uncertain about a plant, nothing quite replaces seeing it in leaf and, ideally, flower. Yet mail-order, internet-based nurseries, such as ours, hope the quality of the stock and the details they provide will fulfil expectations. And they are often the only source for an unusual, treasured variety.

LARGE OR SMALL PLANTS?

When buying plants, size really doesn't matter. As long as a plant is well grown, preferably in a non-peat based compost, a small specimen in a 9cm-square pot can be just as successful as a bigger one in a 2-litre container, especially when planted in the spring. Some perennials are better bought bare-rooted, namely *Iris*, *Paeonia*, and *Phlox*. These all resent being confined in a pot of any size for more than a few months.

Once you've got your new treasures home, make sure they are kept watered, but not wet. Also, don't put them in a greenhouse, which will simply encourage soft top growth and increase the plants' susceptibility to fungal diseases. And there's no rush. I have a cluster of plants in pots outside waiting for a home. Depending on the time of year, they can be fine for a few months.

PREPARING THE SOIL

Whether you prepare the soil before or after you get the plants is up to you. The most important task, whether you are creating a small patch or a big border, is to ensure all perennial weeds are removed. Planting a lovely perennial only to find couch grass making its way through the pretty foliage is annoying. If you feel a need to test the soil for nutrients, now is the moment. It's also the time to add well-rotted manure or garden compost to feed and enrich the soil.

PLOTTING

Before I plant up a large area or border, I draw a plan on a piece of paper. This helps me to get an idea of the overall scheme and put the right plants together. But I am not a trained garden designer so my schemes are not what you would call precise. I don't mark the exact planting spots on the plan and I tend to estimate the number of plants required. What I always do first is to lay out the plants in their pots on the ground. Of course, you need to have some idea of how wide a plant will grow, but a basic rule of thumb is three perennials per square metre, and it seems to be a good guide. With big, tall plants, such as *Eupatorium*, I use just one or two plants per square metre. With smaller plants, such as *Senecio polypodon*, four plants will fit in the same space. The wider the plant, the fewer are needed.

Once all the plants are spaced out, I walk away then go back a day later to check I'm still happy with the arrangement. If all is well, the plants are put into the ground (usually by my husband). This system works best when there is some foliage or flower colour showing to aid the design.

PLANTING

Having dug the hole, put the plant in and back fill. I always water once plants are in the ground, even if it is raining. Then a label goes in, next to the plant, pushed far enough into the ground to stop it being blown away by the wind. It reminds me what the plant is, as well as where it is, especially if it dies back over winter.

IMMEDIATE AFTERCARE

It is important, particularly with newly planted borders, to keep weeds at bay. I love using my hoe, but in chunky clay soil like ours it can be hard work. Don't, however, neglect this chore; it will pay dividends later. Keep newly planted perennials watered for the first few days – longer if the weather is very dry. It will get the roots off to a good start and help them establish more quickly.

Make sure the new beds are cleared of weeds

Nurseries are often the best source of good-quality as well as unusual plants

Planting out after positioning pots

Once perennials have settled, in most cases there isn't much more to be done. Every three weeks or so, between May and October, I have a good look at everything, especially any new plantings.

STAKING

As perennials grow, those with large flowers, such as peonies, may need support to keep the flowers upright. This may not be necessary in the first year, but in later years when the flowers get bigger and heavier, you may need to stake the stems using hoops or canes. Put supports in early in the season as you will be less likely to damage the plant. The stems will also grow through and disguise their supports. Plants that topple over in high wind or heavy rain will also need support and short hoops are a great help.

DIVIDING

There are three reasons for dividing perennials: to increase the number of plants, to reduce the size of a plant, or to make it more vigorous. The method is the same, but the time to do this may vary. Most should, or can, be lifted and split every three years or so. Bear in mind that the growth of fast-growing perennials such as *Aster*, *Campanula*, *Geranium*, and *Nepeta* lessens as the plant gets older. Very tall plants, such as *Echinops* and *Eupatorium*, also use a lot of energy, but they can be reduced in size to keep them tidy. However, long-lived, slow-growing plants such as *Paeonia* are better left in situ for many years.

The time to divide a plant is once the foliage has died back in autumn. Cut off the old top growth, lift the plant out using a fork, then

The stems of *Paeonia* 'Coral Charm' are so tall they may need staking

The back garden in winter

Geranium 'Blue Cloud' trimmed back (with helper)

Geranium 'Blue Cloud' a few weeks after cutting back

knock as much soil off the roots as you can. Set the plant on a stable surface and use a large carving knife to cut through it. I have never done it, but you can use two border forks placed back to back to prise a mature, clumping perennial with large roots apart.

The divisions should not be too small, although this depends on the plant. After three years, the crown of some perennials can be up to 30cm across. Dividing these might yield 20 plants or more, but the sections would probably be very small. It's best to create larger divisions with lots of healthy shoots and strong roots. This should provide you with enough sections to replant with some over to give away. You can then discard the old, woody central section.

FERTILISING

I rarely feed my perennnial plantings, not through any unwillingness but because it doesn't often cross my mind. Perennials' native habitats tend to be rough, wild areas so, in the main, they don't require much feeding. Overfeed them and many produce lots of top growth and no flowers. However, if your border hasn't been touched for some years, it may well benefit from a sprinkling of granular fertiliser in spring or autumn. Incorporating well-rotted farmyard manure or home-made garden compost into the soil is even more beneficial. Just don't overdo it: too much feeding will result in giants or heavy, floppy plants.

DEAD-HEADING AND CUTTING BACK

I do try and cut off dead flowers as they fade throughout the summer, concentrating my efforts on those plants that look really untidy. It's best to take off the flowering stem, not just the individual dead flowers. Removing flowering stems and cutting back the foliage to ground level also helps certain plants produce fresh growth and sometimes more flowers. These include *Achillea*, *Astrantia* (but not *A. maxima*), *Centaurea*, *Echinops*, and *Geranium*. Trimming back also keeps the plant tidy if it becomes unruly.

In late autumn, I begin to cut perennials back once the old leaves and stems have turned brown. Initially I choose only the tattiest plants; the neatest, most upright will provide interest and structure for many months until winter winds flatten them. Cutting back proper starts in spring, anytime between late February and March, just before new growth emerges. I also remove any weeds beneath the old stems to clean the ground for the summer to come.

Paeonia 'Lord Kitchener' produces lots of seeds, but it will only come true when divided

The best way to propagate *Papaver orientale* 'Black and White' is to take root cuttings

Astrantia seeds are plentiful

Rather than buying perennials, which can be costly, you can propagate them yourself. Division from a mother plant or sowing seed are the easiest methods. Root and stem cuttings can be a matter of trial and error, but nothing ventured, nothing gained.

Divisions and runners

Almost all perennials can be divided and this will also keep them vigorous. The best time to divide a plant is during its dormant period, from autumn to spring. For advice on how to do this, *see* Dividing on p. 31. Some plants have roots that run, such as *Geranium macrorrhizum*, while others, like *Ajuga*, produce runners. To propagate both these plants, simply pull off pieces of the plant that have roots and pot them up.

Root cuttings

Some plants are best propagated from root cuttings. These include *Papaver, Echinops, Eryngium,* and *Phlox*. Lift the plant when dormant and, with a clean knife, cut a healthy piece of root into lengths of about 7cm. Cutting the bottom of the root at an angle will remind you to put this end in first. Then make a hole, using a pencil, in a deep pot of free-draining compost and sink the root, angled-end down, into it. If you have lots of roots, put them into a polythene bag with ample moist compost, and roll it up. Leave the pot or polythene bag in a shady place, sheltered from the rain, until green shoots appear in spring.

Seeds

I love collecting and sowing seeds. It is easy and very satisfying. Seeds form all summer, so keep your eyes open and as soon as a pod forms or the flower turns brown, cut the stem off. Do this on a dry day and store the whole stem upside down in a paper bag (don't use plastic: the seeds will sweat and then rot). The seeds should drop off easily; if they don't give them a good rattle. Seeds can be sown at any time, but I usually choose February – a month when little else happens. Sow them into a tray of peat-free, potting compost and cover them according to the size of the seed. Small seeds need very little covering; just enough compost to stop them drying out. Tiny seeds, such as *Digitalis*, can simply be watered in; large seeds, such as *Lupinus*, can be pushed in.

Keep the compost moist, but not wet and place outside or in a cool greenhouse. Germination depends on the plant, but it can be slow. Don't give up until you are absolutely sure nothing is left growing in the tray; you might miss that last gem.

PERENNIALS TO RAISE FROM SEED

Those listed below are usually grown from seed, but remember that named varieties will not come true from seed. Plants with a single asterisk are, in my experience, slow to germinate; those with two are also difficult.

Agastache	*Lathyrus*
Alchemilla	*Lupinus*
*Astrantia**	*Lychnis*
*Baptisia**	*Morina*
Campanula	*Phlomis**
Centaurea	*Pimpinella***
*Delphinium**	*Primula**
*Dictamnus***	*Rudbeckia*
Digitalis	*Sanguisorba**
Echinacea	*Selinum*
Echinops	*Senecio*
*Eryngium**	*Stachys*
*Eupatorium**	*Stokesia**
Euphorbia	*Succisa*
Geranium	*Thalictrum**
Geum	*Thermopsis**
*Gillenia**	*Uvularia***
*Helleborus***	*Valeriana*
Knautia	*Verbena*
*Lamium orvala**	*Veronica**

Stem cuttings

I propagate *Anthemis* and *Dianthus* from stem cuttings; it is possible to use the same method with *Delphinium* and *Lupinus* but they are difficult. Take cuttings in March or April, when the plant is in full growth. The short off-shoots, found at the leaf junctions, are suitable for cutting. Carefully tear off those shoots that are quite large and preferably without flower buds. If there are buds, pinch them out. Then trim the base straight with a sharp, clean knife and poke it into a pot of moistened, but well-drained compost. Cover the pot with a polythene bag to prevent the cuttings from drying out and place on a windowsill or in a greenhouse – somewhere not too hot.

LONGEVITY

It is fairly safe to say that perennials which grow very easily from seed do not live for long. You only have to look at *Echinacea purpurea* to discover that it grows very easily from seed, which is why it is not long-lived. A plant that produces large quantities of seed uses up a lot of energy, but I've found that if you remove the seedheads, the plant can live for longer. By contrast, plants that are difficult to raise from seed, such as *Paeonia* and *Dictamnus*, naturally live for a long time. Growing these plants from seed is difficult and time consuming, therefore they are better raised from divisions.

Snails sometimes eat iris leaves

Silkies in the garden

Mullein moth caterpilllars on *Verbascum*

INSECTS AND OTHER PESTS

The leaves and flowers of perennials are soft and lush, which makes them more prone to attack by insects and other garden pests than to disease. These are the main culprits:

Aphids

It is a fact of gardening that aphids – both green and black – will appear in great quantities to feast on certain plants. Lupins, for instance, are a favourite. Either spray them with an insecticide or squash them by hand to reduce numbers. Do nothing and the whole plant will be weakened.

Caterpillars

I find the only perennial that really suffers from caterpillars is *Verbascum*, which has its very own predator. The caterpillars of the mullein moth – creamy-white with yellow and black markings – graze on the emerging flower stems, stunting the growth. I leave them alone: not only are they attractive to look at, but once they have turned into chrysalises, the plant sends up more flower stems and recovers. If these pests really annoy you, remove them by hand or if you must, spray with an insecticide.

Slugs and snails

These voracious pests tend to home in on precious plants – particularly those growing in a shady, damp place. They also trawl their way up the leaves of irises. Slugs always seem to lurk in grass, while snails hide under vegetation. Pellets can be applied, but they get washed away in rain, and picking slugs off by hand is unpleasant. You can sink a pot of beer in the ground, and it does work for a while, but my own solution – and I realise it's not for everyone – is to keep hens. Small, decorative hens, such as bantams, love slugs and snails, and won't trash the garden. Also, encourage thrushes and hedgehogs – good slug and snail predators – into the garden.

Vine weevils

If you grow a plant in a pot for too long, especially a *Heuchera*, you are likely to encourage vine weevils. Evidence is easy to see: the adults nibble the edge of the leaves, while the larvae eat the roots. Once a plant has been attacked, it's best to discard it.

ANIMAL PESTS

While beneficial insects are welcome in the garden, some mammals are best kept out. Rabbits and deer are two that can cause considerable damage to certain perennials. Deer don't try to eat our garden plants but rabbits do. The only way to deter rabbits is to erect a physical barrier round your garden. Put up a fence and bury the wire netting below ground to stop rabbits tunnelling underneath. You can also avoid growing plants they like. Plants listed below are not foolproof – certain rabbits will eat anything – but worth a try.

RABBIT-PROOF PLANTS

Aconitum	*Iris*
Alchemilla	*Kniphofia*
Anemone	*Lamium*
Aquilegia	*Lysimachia*
Aster	*Miscanthus*
Astilbe	*Nepeta*
Bergenia	*Paeonia*
Campanula lactiflora	*Papaver*
Crocosmia	*Persicaria*
Digitalis	*Polygonatum*
Epimedium	*Pulmonaria*
Eupatorium	*Sedum*
Helenium	*Tellima*
Helianthus	*Tradescantia*
Helleborus × *hybridus*	*Trillium*

DISEASES

Most perennials are trouble free and suffer from very few diseases. These are the principal complaints:

Leaf spot

Dark spots on leaves on very hot summer days after early rain are usually the result of leaf scorch. Spots that appear during milder weather are likely to be symptoms of the fungal disease leaf spot. Hellebores and irises are prone, especially if the weather is warm and damp, or in autumn when the plants are beginning to die back. The best option is to remove and destroy affected leaves. Having said that, I've never had a perennial die because of leaf spot.

Mildew

Mildew can be a pain, especially later in summer when the weather is warm and wet. The first symptom is a fine silver-grey film on the leaves. *Monarda* and Michaelmas-daisy types of *Aster* often suffer from mildew, as do *Stachys byzantina*, *Pulmonaria*, some hardy geraniums, and *Aquilegia*. According to one theory, the disease is more prevalent in dry soils, yet it also affects plants that grow in our moist clay loam. The best solution is to cut the whole plant back to encourage new, stronger growth.

The Perennial Directory

The following pages are dedicated to the plants I love, and these are all plants I would not be without. The sections on *Iris* and *Paeonia* are unashamedly long because over the years I have grown hundreds of varieties. There are far too many to include all of them here so I've chosen the most reliable hybrids and my current favourites. In years to come these might alter.

The information given in each main entry appears as follows:

- **ACHILLEA** This is the family name of the plant.
- (Yarrow) The common name appears after the family in brackets.
- An overall description of the family follows.
- **Needs** The amount of sun and drainage plants in this family generally require.
- **Great for** The best place in the border to grow the plants.
- **Bees & Butterflies** Indicates whether the plants attract these beneficial insects.
- **For Cutting** Indicates which plants make good cut flowers.
- **Care** Advice and tips that will help you grow the plants successfully.
- **'Credo'** or *filpendulina* **'Gold Plate'** The name of the cultivar or variety is in bold after the family name.
- The flowering periods are given in months except for *Iris* and *Paeonia*, which are designated 'Early', 'Mid', and 'Late'.
- **H x S** tells you the height and spread of the plant.
- **AGM** Included at the end of certain plant entries, this stands for 'Award of Garden Merit'. It is given by the Royal Horticultural Society to plants grown in trials over some years that are judged to have fulfilled certain criteria, such as disease resistance. The trials can be limited, but they are a useful guide to performance, and an AGM can be taken to signify a good garden plant. No AGM awards have been included for irises or peonies because these plant groups are being re-assessed.

The back border at White Hopton Farm, in June. In front (from left to right) are *Campanula lactiflora*, *Geranium* 'Brookside', *Centranthus ruber*. On the other side of grass (right to left) *Geranium* 'Orion', *Campanula persicifolia* 'Cornish Mist', *Geranium* 'Nimbus', and *Gillenia trifoliata* are in full bloom.

Acanthus mollis

Acanthus spinosus

Achillea 'Credo'

Achillea 'Fanal'

Achillea filipendulina 'Gold Plate'

Achillea 'Forncett Fletton'

ACANTHUS

These stately plants add a touch of grandness to a border. Both varieties produce white flowers with two floppy lips that shelter under a shell-like purple hood. The flowers are carried up a sturdy stem to form a thick spike that rises elegantly from a broad, slowly spreading clump of leaves.

Needs Well-drained soil in sun or partial shade
Great for Middle or back of a border
Bees & Butterflies No
For Cutting Yes
Care Long-lived, resistant to drought. Can be difficult to eradicate once established

mollis (Bear's breeches) A vigorous plant with big, sculpted, dark green, shiny leaves. June to August. **H × S** 150cm × 90cm

spinosus (Armed bear's breeches) More deeply divided leaves than *A. mollis*; each leaf division is tipped with a little pin. June to August. **H × S** 120cm × 90cm

ACHILLEA (Yarrow)

Excellent for adding layers of horizontal colour to a border, achilleas perfectly complement clump-forming plants. Each broad head is made up of smaller flowers and carried on stiff stems above long, deeply divided, often feathery leaves. The flowers of some varieties change colour as they open. Most last well, creating a layered effect of two-tone colour.

Needs Well-drained soil in sun
Great for Front or middle of the border
Bees & Butterflies Yes
For Cutting Yes
Care Remove faded flowers to encourage more, leaving the last blooms to add strong shape to the border throughout winter.

'Credo' A gentle plant with upright stems of soft-yellow flowers and mid-green, feathery leaves. June to September. **H × S** 90cm × 60cm. AGM

'Fanal' Bright pink-red, richly coloured flowers fade to brick-red with age. The leaves are feathery and mid-green. Sometimes sold as 'The Beacon'. June to September. **H × S** 60cm × 30cm

filipendulina **'Gold Plate'** Stiffly upright stems are topped with shallow-domed heads of bright-yellow flowers above neatly divided, grey-green leaves. July to September. **H × S** 120cm × 90cm. AGM

'Forncett Fletton' The flowers open soft red and become orange as the centres get bigger. The feathery leaves are grey-green. June to September. **H × S** 75cm × 60cm *millefolium* **'Lilac Beauty'** A pretty, two-tone plant with soft lilac-pink flowers fading to almost white over time and carried above a mound of fluffy, lush green leaves. June to September. **H × S** 70cm × 45cm

millefolium **'Red Velvet'** Unlike many red varieties, its blooms do not fade as they age. The broad heads of rich-red flowers combine beautifully with soft grey-green leaves to create a neat mounding plant. June to September. **H × S** 75cm × 60cm

'Moonshine' Small heads of sulphur-yellow flowers are carried on well-branched, grey stems above evergreen, soft-grey leaves to from an open, domed mound. July to September. **H × S** 60cm × 45cm. AGM

'Paprika' A variety with flowers that open scarlet and fade to a paler red. The leaves are finely divided and grey-green. June to September. **H × S** 70cm × 60cm

'Terracotta' Ideal for hot borders, the heads of burnt-orange flowers turn rich yellow with age and are carried on stiffly upright stems with soft, grey-green leaves. June to September. **H × S** 75cm × 60cm

'Walther Funcke' Heads of red flowers, each with a yellow eye, fade to tangerine-orange. A good upright plant with feathery, grey-green foliage. June to September. **H × S** 60cm × 45cm

Achillea millefolium 'Lilac Beauty'

Achillea 'Moonshine'

Achillea millefolium 'Red Velvet'

Achillea 'Paprika'

Achillea 'Terracotta'

Achillea 'Walther Funcke'

ACONITUM (Monkshood)

These dignified, upright plants are a great alternative, if a little shorter in stature, to delphiniums in gardens where slugs are a problem. The flowers are really small and hidden under helmet-shaped hoods. Aconitums generally produce tall spikes with deeply divided, shiny, rather leathery, deep-green leaves at the base. They spread slowly into a substantial clump.

Needs Well-drained soil in sun or partial shade
Great for Middle or back of the border
Bees & Butterflies Bees
For Cutting Yes
Care All parts are poisonous so wear gloves when handling. After flowering, the entire plant dies back, leaving only the tuberous roots. Feed in spring to keep it vigorous

'Bressingham Spire' An elegant plant that produces slender columns of deep indigo-blue flowers. July to September. **H × S** 90cm × 50cm. AGM

× cammarum 'Bicolor' The white flowers are broadly stained along the edges with violet. Carried on short branches, they form a thick, upright spire. June to August. **H × S** 120cm × 60cm. AGM

carmichaelii 'Arendsii' A late-flowering plant that produces dumpy spikes of rich-blue flowers. Perhaps the easiest variety to grow. August to October. **H × S** 120cm × 60cm. AGM

'Spark's Variety' A 'see-through' plant with deep violet-blue flowers carried on well-spaced, slender side branches above deeply divided, glossy, dark green leaves. June to August. **H × S** 150cm × 90cm. AGM

Aconitum × *cammarum* 'Bicolor'

Aconitum 'Bressingham Spire'

Aconitum carmichaelii 'Arendsii'

Aconitum 'Spark's Variety'

ACTAEA (Bugbane)

Graceful, majestic, and eye-catching, the long, slender, bottle brush-like spikes of tiny, scented, white flowers turn fluffy as the stamens emerge. The seed pods are also decorative. Flower spikes are carried on slender stems above an elegant, open clump of deeply divided leaves that hold themselves proudly. Many dark-leaved varieties look similar.

Needs As long as soil remains moist, will grow in sun and partial or near-total shade
Great for Woodland and shady spots
Bees & Butterflies Bees
For Cutting Yes
Care Dark-leaved varieties may scorch in bright sunlight. Can be slow to establish

racemosa (Black cohosh) This has lacy, bright-green leaves forming an open clump. July. **H × S** 120cm × 75cm. AGM

simplex **Atropurpurea Group** A plant with dark flower stems and dark purple leaves. August to October. **H × S** 150cm × 75cm

simplex **Atropurpurea Group 'Brunette'** The leaves are really dark maroon, almost black. August to October. **H × S** 150cm × 75cm. AGM

simplex **Atropurpurea Group 'James Compton'** The darkest leaved of the Atropurpurea Group varieties with perfect spikes of white flowers. August to October. **H × S** 150cm × 75cm. AGM

AGASTACHE (Giant hyssop)

Upright, bushy plants with long, fat spikes of small flowers that resemble those of mint and are loved by bees. These are carried on stiff stems with aromatic, light-green leaves that when crushed have a scent similar to that of liquorice.

Needs Well-drained soil in sun or partial shade
Great for Middle of a border
Bees & Butterflies Yes
For Cutting No
Care Trouble free but liable to seed about

'Blue Fortune' Raised from seed, this variety has soft violet-blue flowers. July to September. **H × S** 90cm × 75cm. AGM

rugosa **f. albiflora** The white flowers poke out of green calyces, making them appear off-white in tone. July to September. **H × S** 90cm × 75cm

Actaea racemosa

Actaea simplex Atropurpurea Group

Actaea simplex Atropurpurea Group 'Brunette'

Actaea simplex Atropurpurea Group 'James Compton'

Agastache 'Blue Fortune'

Agastache rugosa f. *albiflora*

Ageratina altissima 'Braunlaub'

Ageratina altissima 'Chocolate'

Ajuga reptans 'Catlin's Giant'

Alchemilla conjuncta

Alchemilla erythropoda

AGERATINA

Formerly listed as *Eupatorium*, these bushy, upright plants start into growth late in spring and flower long after most perennials have gone over. The flowers form small balls with fluffy stamens and are held in shallow domed heads on well-branched stems with oval leaves.

Needs Moist soil in sun or partial shade
Great for Middle of a border
Bees & Butterflies Bees
For Cutting No
Care Trouble free in the right soil

altissima **'Braunlaub'** Fluffy white heads are carried just above a leafy, upright clump of oval, mid-green leaves. August to October. **H × S** 90cm × 75cm

altissima **'Chocolate'** The deep purple-brown leaves form a handsome bushy clump that is more useful and attractive in a border than the off-white flowers. August to October. **H × S** 90cm × 75cm

AJUGA (Bugle)

reptans **'Catlin's Giant'** A ground-hugging plant with broad, stumpy spikes of large, bright-blue flowers similar to those of mint. These are held above a dense carpet of big, leathery, evergreen, shiny, purple leaves. April to June. **H × S** 15cm × 45cm. AGM

Needs If the soil retains moisture, will tolerate sun right through to shade
Great for Edging borders
Bees & Butterflies No
For Cutting No
Care May suffer from mildew

ALCHEMILLA (Lady's mantle)

A discreet and undemanding plant that is invaluable for its ground-covering mounds of interesting, scalloped leaves and loose, airy heads of greenish-yellow flowers.

Needs Well-drained soil in sun or partial shade
Great for Edges of borders
Bees & Butterflies No
For Cutting Yes
Care Remove flowers before they set seed if you don't want an invasion of plants

conjuncta Clusters of lime-green flowers sprout from shiny, deep-green leaves that are silver below and edged with a fine, silver line. July to August. **H × S** 30cm × 30cm

erythropoda A small, tidy plant with matt, mid-green leaves and small sprays of lime-green flowers. June to September. **H × S** 15cm × 30cm. AGM

mollis Lacy sprays of tiny, yellow-green flowers on long stems spill out from a mound of large, round, soft-green leaves. May to August. **H × S** 60cm × 75cm. AGM

AMSONIA (Blue star)

tabernaemontana* var. *salicifolia An open, upright plant with stiff, slender, almost black stems. These carry sprays of small, starry, pale-blue flowers towards the top. The shiny, soft-green, willow-like leaves are handsome and turn yellow in autumn. July to August. **H × S** 75cm × 60cm

Needs Well-drained soil in sun or partial shade
Great for Middle of a border
Bees & Butterflies No
For Cutting No
Care Slow to establish, but long-lived

ANAPHALIS

triplinervis A plant that harmonises easily with other perennials. It forms a broad dome with long stems of soft, felted, grey leaves and sprays of small, double white flowers that are papery to the touch. July to August. **H × S** 75cm × 60cm. AGM

Needs Well-drained soil that retains moisture in sun
Great for Front and middle of the border
Bees & Butterflies Yes
For Cutting Yes
Care Trouble free in the right soil

ANCHUSA (Alkanet)

***azurea* 'Loddon Royalist'** Very few perennials offer such vivid blue flowers. Small and bright, they are carried in a spike on tall, hairy, reddish stems above a basal clump of long, hairy, mid-green leaves. May to July. **H × S** 90cm × 75cm

Needs Well-drained soil that remains moist, but not boggy, in sun or partial shade
Great for Back of the border
Bees & Butterflies No
For Cutting No
Care In wet soils the roots will rot. Remove old flower stems to encourage more blooms

Alchemilla mollis

Amsonia tabernaemontana var. *salicifolia*

Anaphalis triplinervis

Anchusa azurea 'Loddon Royalist'

Anemone hupehensis 'Hadspen Abundance'

Anemone hupehensis var. *japonica* 'Pamina'

Anemone hupehensis var. *japonica*
'Prinz Heinrich'

Anemone hupehensis 'Praecox'

Anemone × *hybrida* 'Honorine Jobert'

Anemone × *hybrida* 'Königin Charlotte'

ANEMONE (Japanese anemone)

A determined, long-lived plant with large, simple blooms carried elegantly on slender, branched stems. Forms colonies of dense mounds of vine-shaped, mid-green leaves. Left on the stem, the seedheads burst open to reveal fluffy seeds that provide food for small birds during the winter months.

Needs Well-drained soil that remains moist in sun or partial shade
Great for Back of the border
Bees & Butterflies Yes
For Cutting Yes
Care After taking a year or two to settle, the plants can be left untouched for years

hupehensis **'Hadspen Abundance'** Single, satiny, deep-pink flowers with pale-pink backs. August to October. **H × S** 90cm × 75cm. AGM.

hupehensis **var.** *japonica* **'Pamina'** Deep-pink, semi-double flowers carried on a network of dark red, wiry stems. August to September. **H × S** 75cm × 60cm. AGM

hupehensis **var.** *japonica* **'Prinz Heinrich'** Ruffled, semi-double, dark pink flowers with slender petals. August to September. **H × S** 90cm × 75cm. AGM

hupehensis **'Praecox'** A tough plant with soft-pink flowers and large leaves that are rough to the touch. August to October. **H × S** 90cm × 90cm

× *hybrida* **'Honorine Jobert'** Single, white flowers. A classically elegant plant. August to September. **H × S** 90cm × 75cm. AGM

× *hybrida* **'Königin Charlotte'** Large, slim-petalled, soft-pink flowers. August to September. **H × S** 90cm × 75cm. AGM

× *hybrida* **'September Charm'** Soft-pink, single flowers, darker underneath, with three larger petals. August to September. **H × S** 90cm × 90cm. AGM

× *hybrida* **'Serenade'** Large, soft lavender-pink, semi-double flowers. August to September. **H × S** 90cm × 80cm

× *hybrida* **'Whirlwind'** Rosette-shaped, pure-white, semi-double flowers. August to September. **H × S** 90cm × 75cm

tomentosa A vigorous plant with open sprays of soft-pink flowers carried on well-branched stems above rough, mid-green leaves. A rather robust plant that once established will spread around. August to October. **H × S** 100cm × 120cm

Anemone × *hybrida* 'September Charm'

Anemone × *hybrida* 'Serenade'

Anemone × *hybrida* 'Whirlwind'

Anemone tomentosa

Anthemis punctata subsp. *cupaniana*

Anthemis tinctoria 'E. C. Buxton'

ANTHEMIS (Chamomile)

These cheerful plants produce a mass of daisy-shaped flowers on slender stems that cover a mound of fragrant, finely cut leaves.

Needs Well-drained soil in sun
Great for *A. tinctoria* types will fill borders quickly. *A. punctata* subsp. *cupaniana* is good for softening the edges of borders, paths, and patios
Bees & Butterflies Yes
For Cutting Yes
Care Cut back in spring

punctata* subsp. *cupaniana Beneath a sea of white daisies lies a tumbling mass of deeply cut grey leaves. May to August. **H × S** 30cm × 75cm. AGM

***tinctoria* 'E. C. Buxton'** Masses of light-lemon flowers are carried on long stems with mid-green leaves. *A. tinctoria* 'Wargrave' is slightly paler in colour. June to August. **H × S** 60cm × 60cm

AQUILEGIA (Columbine, Granny's bonnet)

This classic cottage-garden plant bears its dangling flowers, which often have short spurs, on slender stems above a mound of lobed, mid-green leaves. Garden plants hybridize with each other producing flowers of varying colours.

Needs Well-drained soil in sun or partial shade
Great for Middle of the border
Bees & Butterflies Bees
For Cutting Yes
Care Will seed freely around the garden

vulgaris A variable plant with blue, white, or pink flowers and short spurs projecting from the back. May to July. **H × S** 75cm × 45cm

Aquilegia vulgaris

Aquilegia vulgaris var. *alba*

Aquilegia vulgaris var. *stellata* 'Nora Barlow'

Aquilegia vulgaris var. *stellata* 'Ruby Port'

Aquilegia vulgaris 'William Guiness'

vulgaris **var.** *alba* Pure-white flowers with short spurs above pale-green leaves. May to July. **H × S** 75cm × 45cm

vulgaris **var.** *stellata* **'Nora Barlow'** A frilly, double, deep-pink variety with paler edges to the petals and no spurs. May to July. **H × S** 75cm × 45cm

vulgaris **var.** *stellata* **'Ruby Port'** A richly coloured plant with deep-red, spurless flowers. May to July. **H × S** 75cm × 45cm

vulgaris **'William Guiness'** Eye-catching black-purple, long-spurred flowers with white edges and centres. May to July. **H × S** 75cm × 45cm

ARTEMISIA

ludoviciana **'Valerie Finnis'** Tall stems of soft-grey leaves with jagged tips form a bushy clump that is topped with insignificant yellow flowers. An excellent if unassuming companion to grow with softly coloured flowers. August to September. **H × S** 60cm × 60cm. AGM

Needs Well-drained soil in sun
Great for Middle of a border
Bees & Butterflies No
For Cutting No
Care Trouble free and ideal for dry soils

ARUNCUS (Goatsbeard)

Although not a colourful perennial, this makes a really impressive plant.

Needs Soil that remains moist in sun, partial shade or shade
Bees & Butterflies No
For Cutting No
Great for Front and back of the border
Care Trouble free, but slow to establish

dioicus A big plant to use as a focal point. Tiny cream flowers form fluffy spikes that rise from a mound of mid-green leaves. June to July. **H × S** 180cm × 150cm. AGM

dioicus **'Kneiffii'** From a mound of gauzy, mid-green leaves, sprays of tiny, cream flowers erupt like a firework on long, arching stems. June to August. **H × S** 60cm × 45cm

ASPHODELINE

lutea (Jacob's rod) A Chelsea favourite, its broad spears of starry, bright-yellow flowers, open at intervals above fine, grassy leaves. May to June. **H × S** 90cm × 45cm

Needs Well-drained soil in sun; best in a hot spot
Great for Middle of the border
Bees & Butterflies Bees
For Cutting Yes
Care Trouble free

Artemisia ludoviciana 'Valerie Finnis'

Aruncus dioicus 'Kneiffii'

Aruncus dioicus

Asphodeline lutea

Aster amellus 'Rosa Erfüllung' (front) with *Persicaria amplexicaulis* 'Taurus' (left) and *Aconitum carmichaelii* 'Arendsii' (right)

ASTER

I cannot overstate the usefulness of these late-flowering plants. The choice is extensive with too many varieties to list here. Some form tight, leafy mounds and some are stiffly upright, while others form open clumps. All produce sprays of daisy-like flowers that will brighten up the dullest of autumn days. The most colourful are the true Michaelmas daisies (*A. novi-belgii*), which some might consider a little too bright. Others are less showy and bloom only in shades of lilac.

Needs Well-drained soil that remains moist in sun
Great for All parts of the border
Bees & Butterflies Yes
For Cutting Yes
Care *A. novi-belgii* types can suffer from mildew in warm, damp years. Otherwise trouble free

amellus **'Rosa Erfüllung'** A stiffly upright plant with open sprays of smallish, pale-pink flowers and soft, mid-green leaves. August to October. **H × S** 60cm × 45cm

'Coombe Fishacre' A really nice plant with small, pale-mauve flowers covering a clump of little, deep-green leaves. September to October. **H × S** 90cm × 60cm. AGM

divaricatus Sprays of small, starry, white flowers rise from an uneven mound of heart-shaped, deep-green leaves. September to October. **H × S** 60cm × 60cm

ericoides **'Pink Cloud'** A broad mounding variety, its long stems are coated with tiny, soft-pink flowers. The slender leaves are mid-green. September to October. **H × S** 60cm × 60cm. AGM

× *frikartii* **'Mönch'** One of the earliest and longest flowering asters, it produces a continuous display of large, single, lilac daisies. The plant forms a neat dome with disease-free, mid-green leaves. August to September. **H × S** 60cm × 60cm. AGM

× *frikartii* **'Wunder von Stäfa'** In colour and foliage, a very similar variety to 'Mönch', although its flowers are larger and the petals are rather unruly. August to September. **H × S** 90cm × 60cm. AGM

glehnii An unusual, very upright aster that, although a little rough around the edges, grows into an airy plant topped with broad clusters of small, white flowers. The leaves are long and pointed. September to November. **H × S** 120cm × 75cm

Aster 'Coombe Fishacre'

Aster divaricatus

Aster ericoides 'Pink Cloud'

Aster × frikartii 'Mönch'

Aster × frikartii 'Wunder von Stäfa'

Aster glehnii

Aster 'Little Carlow'

Aster lateriflorus 'Prince'

Aster novae-angliae
'Andenken an Alma Pötschke'

lateriflorus **'Prince'** A tight, bushy plant with tiny, dark green leaves and stiff branches coated with small, white, pink-centred flowers. October to November. **H × S** 90cm × 75cm

'Little Carlow' A lovely aster with hefty sprays of bright, mid-blue flowers and mid-green leaves. September to October. **H × S** 90cm × 75cm. AGM

Aster novae-angliae (New England asters) *Plants in this group produce colourful clusters of flowers at the top of stiffly upright stems, which become bare at the base. Their rough leaves do not suffer from mildew.*

novae-angliae **'Andenken an Alma Pötschke'** Tight clusters of bright cerise-pink autumn blooms adorn this tall variety. September to November. **H × S** 120cm × 75cm

novae-angliae **'Harrington's Pink'** A neat variety with soft-pink flowers. September to November. **H × S** 120cm × 75cm. AGM

novae-angliae **'Herbstschnee'** The single pure-white flowers are carried on stiffly upright stems. September to November. **H × S** 120cm × 75cm

novae-angliae **'Purple Dome'** A short, late-season plant with rich-purple flowers. One of the last New England asters to flower. September to November. **H × S** 60cm × 45cm

Aster novi-belgii (Michaelmas daisies) *Of all the asters, these bear the brightest, most colourful flowers on slim, stiff stems. The shiny, deep-green leaves can suffer from mildew.*

novi-belgii **'Jenny'** A short plant with single, deep pink-red flowers covering a dome of dark green, shiny leaves. September to October. **H × S** 30cm × 30cm

novi-belgii **'Lady In Blue'** A free-flowering, short plant with single, violet-blue flowers. September to October. **H × S** 30cm × 30cm

novi-belgii **'Marie Ballard'** A tall plant with double, soft lilac-blue flowers. September to October. **H × S** 90cm × 75cm

novi-belgii **'Patricia Ballard'** The double, violet flowers are borne on tall stems. September to October. **H × S** 90cm × 75cm

pyrenaeus **'Lutetia'** Large, single, lilac flowers tumble out in a mass of stars to form a low, spreading clump with slender, mid-green leaves. September to October. **H × S** 75cm × 70cm

'Wood's Pink' A neatly domed plant covered with small, lilac-pink flowers. September to October. **H × S** 30cm × 30cm

Aster novae-angliae 'Harrington's Pink'

Aster novae-angliae 'Herbstschnee'

Aster novae-angliae 'Purple Dome'

Aster novi-belgii 'Jenny'

Aster novi-belgii 'Lady In Blue'

Aster novi-belgii 'Marie Ballard'

Aster novi-belgii 'Patricia Ballard'

Aster 'Wood's Pink'

Aster pyrenaeus 'Lutetia'

Astilbe 'Betsy Cuperus'

Astilbe 'Fanal'

ASTILBE

Tidy in their growing habit, astilbes carry fluffy spikes of tiny flowers on slender stems above a decorative mound of deeply divided leaves. They will grow in any soil that does not dry out, but are most useful in wet soils or around the edge of a pond. The flower colours can be on the bold side, which makes it difficult to mix them with other perennials, but they look good planted in groups.

Needs Soil that remains very moist: wet clay, boggy soils or beside a stream or pond
Great for Wet, shady areas
Bees & Butterflies Yes
For Cutting Yes
Care Trouble-free in the right soil

'Betsy Cuperus' (× *thunbergii*) Tiny, soft-pink flowers form loose spikes on long stems that arch elegantly over divided, pale-green leaves. July to August **H × S** 120cm × 90cm

chinensis **'Vision in Red'** Flowering for longer than other varieties, it bears slim, fluffy, purple-red blooms. These open from rich-red buds high above the deep-green leaves. July to August. **H × S** 45cm × 45cm

'Fanal' (× *arendsii*) Open plumes of bright-scarlet flowers on red stems rise above a neat mound of leaves. The foliage contrasts handsomely with the flowers. July to August. **H × S** 30cm × 30cm. AGM

'Weisse Gloria' (× *arendsii*) A free-flowering hybrid with candy-floss spikes of creamy-white flowers carried above a compact mound of mid-green leaves. July to August. **H × S** 75cm × 60cm

Astilbe chinensis 'Vision In Red'

Astilbe 'Weisse Gloria'

ASTRANTIA (Masterwort)

Among the loveliest border perennials, their distinctive, papery flowers look like small pin cushions. These are carried in upright sprays on wiry, branched stems above a mound of deeply cut leaves. When I started in the nursery trade there were just a few varieties, but astrantias readily cross pollinate so there are now many more to choose from. Some are very similar – so similar it is difficult to tell the difference.

Needs Given well-drained soil that remains moist, will grow in sun, partial shade, and even fairly shady spots
Great for Middle of a border
Bees & Butterflies Yes
For Cutting Yes
Care Cut back (except *A. maxima*) after flowering to prevent the plant seeding around and to encourage more flowers

'Buckland' One of the earliest- and longest- flowering varieties with soft, dusky-pink flowers and mid-green leaves. May to July. **H × S** 60cm × 50cm

'Hadspen Blood' Rich-red flowers are produced above deep-green foliage, and the leaves are also highlighted with red. June to August. **H × S** 60cm × 45cm

major Flower size varies, but the colour is white, often tinged with pink. The leaves are mid-green. May to July. **H × S** 90cm × 60cm

'Roma' An excellent variety with glowing, rich-pink flowers and mid-green leaves. Performs really well in a shady spot. May to September. **H × S** 75cm × 50cm

Astrantia 'Roma'

Astrantia 'Buckland'

Astrantia 'Hadspen Blood'

Astrantia major

Astrantia major 'Claret' with *Digitalis lutea* and *Geum* 'Prinses Juliana'

major **'Claret'** Not the most vigorous variety, this has very dark red flowers on near-black stems and red-tinted, dark green leaves. May to July. **H × S** 60cm × 50cm

major subsp. *involucrata* **'Shaggy'** Good-sized white flowers are surrounded by large bracts that are elegantly tipped with green. The leaves are mid-green. May to August. **H × S** 90cm × 50cm. AGM

major var. *rosea* A variable seed-raised plant with very pale-pink flowers and mid-green leaves. May to July. **H × S** 75cm × 50cm

major **'Rubra'** The easiest red-flowered variety to grow, it bears pure, deep-maroon flowers and has dark green leaves. May to July. **H × S** 60cm × 50cm

major **'Ruby Wedding'** Although rather slow to multiply, when fully established this variety produces handsome, dark ruby-red flowers on red stems with reddish, deep-green leaves. May to July. **H × S** 60cm × 45cm

major **'Sunningdale Variegated'** This plant is especially handsome in spring when the young foliage emerges. At first light green and heavily splashed with soft yellow, the leaves turn mid-green when the stems of white flowers appear. May to August. **H × S** 90cm × 50cm. AGM

maxima The last astrantia to bloom, this plant bears lovely, large, dusky-pink flowers. The mid-green leaves are not as divided as those of the *A. major* group. If not grown in soil that is reliably damp, however, it can be the slowest to multiply. May to July. **H × S** 60cm × 55cm. AGM

Astrantia major var. *rosea*

Astrantia major 'Rubra'

Astrantia major 'Ruby Wedding'

Astrantia major 'Sunningdale Variegated'

Astrantia major subsp. *involucrata* 'Shaggy'

Astrantia maxima

Baptisia australis

Bergenia 'Beethoven'

Bergenia 'Bressingham White'

Bergenia ciliata 'Dumbo'

Bergenia 'Eric Smith'

Bergenia 'Eroica'

BAPTISIA (False indigo)

australis An elegant, upright plant with slender stems of well-spaced, small, indigo-blue, pea-like flowers reminiscent of lupins. Below the flowers round, soft-green leaves are arranged in alternating pairs to the very bottom of the stems. These look good long after the flowers have faded. June to July. **H × S** 90cm × 60cm. AGM

Needs Well-drained soil in sun
Great for Middle of the border
Bees & Butterflies Yes
For Cutting No
Care Remove old flower stems for neatness. May take a little while to establish

BERGENIA (Elephant's ears)

Evergreen perennials are few in number, making these tough plants extra special. Invaluable for suppressing weeds, they form a thick, ground-covering clump of large, leathery, spatula- or spoon-shaped leaves. In spring, sturdy flower stems rise up, topped with fist-like buds that open into clusters of bell-shaped flowers. From autumn to spring the leaves of some varieties are heavily tinged with red or burnished with bronze.

Needs Well-drained soil in sun to shade
Great for Evergreen ground cover. Also good in a pot
Bees & Butterflies No
For Cutting Yes; flowers and leaves
Care Remove old leaves as they die and divide plants when woody growth appears in the centre to keep them neat

'Beethoven' A free-flowering plant with oval, deep-green leaves and towering clusters of white flowers that may turn pink with age. The leaves turn red in autumn. March to April. **H × S** 40cm × 45cm

'Bressingham White' One of the cleanest white varieties with bell-like flowers and long, broad, deep-green leaves. March to April. **H × S** 40cm × 45cm. AGM

ciliata **'Dumbo'** A plant worth growing for the leaves alone, which are large, round, deep-green and hairy. Once the clusters of rather unremarkable pink flowers die, the leaves get bigger, standing up just like a baby elephant's ears. March to April. **H × S** 30cm × 75cm

'Eric Smith' A really pretty plant with small clusters of soft-pink flowers and excellent large, round leaves that become bronze-red with the approach of winter. March to April. **H × S** 40cm × 60cm. AGM

'Eroica' Taller than most bergenias, this also looks good in a container, producing sprays of rich magenta-pink bells on red stems. These bloom above a clump of upright, smooth, oval, deep-green leaves that turn a rich red in autumn. Sometimes sold under the name of 'Overture'. March to May. **H × S** 45cm × 30cm. AGM

'Pink Dragonfly' A free-flowering plant with open, pure-pink flowers cascading from red stems above small, oval, deep-green leaves. A particularly good variety for pots as well as the border. March to September. **H × S** 30cm × 30cm

BRUNNERA (Siberian bugloss)

The large, rough-textured, heart-shaped leaves grow into a dense mound that is covered for weeks with open sprays of little, forget-me-not blue flowers. The leaves remain in good shape well into autumn, covering the ground thickly enough to reduce weed growth.

Needs Well-drained soil in sun or partial shade. If grown in a sunny spot the soil needs to retain some moisture, but in shadier areas plants tolerate fairly dry soils
Great for Shady areas, especially in woodland
Bees & Butterflies Bees
For Cutting Yes, but short-lived
Care Trouble free in the right soil

macrophylla The original green-leaved species, it forms a large, mounding dome covered with sprays of simple, soft-blue flowers. April to June. **H × S** 60cm × 75cm

macrophylla **'Hadspen Cream'** A very handsome plant, especially when seen from a distance. The mid-green leaves are edged with cream; the flowers are blue. April to June. **H × S** 60cm × 75cm. AGM

macrophylla **'Jack Frost'** Perhaps the best of the silver-leaved varieties. With their heavy covering of silver, the handsome green-veined leaves make a lovely backdrop for the sprays of soft-blue flowers. April to June. **H × S** 60cm × 75cm. AGM

macrophylla **'Looking Glass'** The leaves are quite remarkable – large, silver-coated and curling back around the edges. They create a wonderful tight mound. The flowers are blue. April to June. **H × S** 60cm × 75cm

macrophylla **'Mister Morse'** Pure-white flowers make this a good variety for brightening up a dark corner of the garden. The attractive mid-green leaves are brushed with silver. April to June. **H × S** 60cm × 75cm

Bergenia 'Pink Dragonfly'

Brunnera macrophylla

Brunnera macrophylla 'Hadspen Cream'

Brunnera macrophylla 'Jack Frost'

Brunnera macrophylla 'Looking Glass'

Brunnera macrophylla 'Mister Morse'

Calamagrostis x acutiflora 'Karl Foerster'

Calamagrostis x acutiflora 'Overdam'

Calamintha grandiflora

Calamintha nepeta

Calamintha nepeta subsp. glandulosa
'Blue Cloud'

Calamintha nepeta subsp. glandulosa
'White Cloud'

CALAMAGROSTIS (Reed grass)

These are some of the most beautiful of all grasses, with dense clumps of fine leaves that stay upright throughout the year. Late in summer tall, slender stems carry delicate plumes of small, tan-coloured flowers. They don't seed around the garden and are tolerant of many situations.

Needs Well-drained soil in sun or partial shade
Great for Back of the border
Bees & Butterflies No
For Cutting No
Care Trouble free. Cut back in spring

× *acutiflora* **'Karl Foerster'** An upright clump of fine, mid-green leaves produces very tall stems topped with slender plumes of soft-brown flowers. The stems remain rigid over a long period. August to November. **H × S** 180cm × 90cm

× *acutiflora* **'Overdam'** A light, airy plant with green leaves striped with white and sprays of pink-tinged flowers. Ideal for a darker spot in the garden. August to November. **H × S** 180cm × 90cm

CALAMINTHA

Similar to *Nepeta* (*see* p. 135) in both style and use, *Calamintha* blooms much later. Spikes of small, mint-like flowers rise from a bushy clump with very fragrant leaves.

Needs Well-drained soil in sun
Great for Front of the border
Bees & Butterflies Yes
For Cutting No
Care *C. nepeta* types are a little slow to get going and may take two years to fill out

grandiflora A bushy plant producing an abundance of lilac-pink flowers that open between small, pale-green leaves on upright stems. June to August. **H × S** 45cm × 45cm

nepeta A neat, broad mound of small, peppermint-scented leaves produces sprays of tiny, pale-pink flowers. A more upright plant than the blue or white varieties below. July to October. **H × S** 45cm × 60cm

nepeta subsp. *glandulosa* **'Blue Cloud'** A long-flowering plant that produces a hazy mound of soft-blue flowers and little, fragrant, shiny leaves. July to October. **H × S** 45cm × 60cm

nepeta subsp. *glandulosa* **'White Cloud'** The aromatic soft-green foliage is less dense than others in the group. Tiny, pure-white flowers open from cream bracts over a long period. July to October. **H × S** 45cm × 60cm

CAMPANULA (Bellflower)

These charming, versatile plants, producing bell-shaped flowers in a variety of white, blue or pink shades, blend effortlessly with all garden perennials. The best varieties for borders are selected from just a few species and most are easy to grow.

Needs Well-drained soil in sun or partial shade
Great for All parts of the border
Bees & Butterflies Yes
For Cutting Some
Care Trouble free. Try removing old blooms to encourage a few more flowers

alliariifolia A plant with little finesse, yet the display of cream bells dangling all the way up tall, slender stems, makes it ideal for the front of the border. The flower stems sprout from a tight mound of rough, soft-green, heart-shaped leaves that tip gently forward to form a wide, but open plant. June to August. **H × S** 60cm × 60cm

'Crystal' A pretty plant with large, pale-lilac, nodding flowers carried up long, leafy stems and blooming over many weeks. June to August. **H × S** 75cm × 60cm

glomerata var. *alba* (Clustered bellflower) Bell-shaped white flowers form tight clusters and whorls of further flowers are carried down the stiff, leafy stems. These rise above a slowly creeping carpet of mid-green leaves. June and July. **H × S** 45cm × 60cm

glomerata **'Caroline'** Held in tight domes, the flowers of this lovely plant are particularly pretty. The lilac bells are edged with a darker tint, although this subtle colouring disappears as the flower opens. June and July. **H × S** 45cm × 60cm. AGM

glomerata **'Superba'** Richly coloured, deep blue-purple bells cluster together on this robust plant. June and July. **H × S** 45cm × 60cm. AGM

lactiflora (Milk bellflower) A billowing, upright, bushy plant carrying clusters of lilac-blue flowers all the way up tall, leafy stems. 'Prichard's Variety' is a lovely dark blue form, but all too often the plant supplied has soft-blue flowers like the seed-grown species listed here. June to August. **H × S** 120cm × 90cm

Campanula alliariifolia

Campanula 'Crystal'

Campanula glomerata var. *alba*

Campanula glomerata 'Caroline'

Campanula glomerata 'Superba'

Campanula lactiflora

Campanula lactiflora 'Alba'

Campanula lactiflora 'Loddon Anna'

***lactiflora* 'Alba'** Large heads of upright, pure-white bells are borne the length of long stems covered in light-green leaves. A big, frothy plant like the others in the *lactiflora* group. June to August. **H × S** 120cm × 90cm. AGM

***lactiflora* 'Loddon Anna'** On this tall, bushy variety, long stems with soft-green leaves bear foaming heads of pretty, lilac-pink flowers. June to August. **H × S** 120cm × 90cm. AGM

latifolia* var. *macrantha Long, rich-blue bells, which look like pixie hats and face upwards, are carried the length of leafy stems. A tall, graceful, bushy plant. June to August. **H × S** 90cm × 60cm

***latiloba* 'Highcliffe Variety'** (Broad-leaved bellflower) Tall stems bearing a few slender leaves are studded with large, open, violet-blue bells. An elegant, sturdy plant. June to August. **H × S** 75cm × 50cm. AGM

persicifolia (Peach-leaved bellflower) Generous quantities of large, mid-blue, cupped blooms are borne on short branches. The slender flower stems rise from a thick, slowly spreading carpet created by the rosettes of long, shiny, deep-green leaves. June to August. **H × S** 90cm × 60cm

persicifolia* var. *alba The cupped, white flowers are carried all the way up slender stems above the mound of deep-green leaves. June to August. **H × S** 90cm × 60cm

Campanula latifolia var. *macrantha*

Campanula latiloba 'Highcliffe Variety'

Campanula persicifolia

Campanula persicifolia var. *alba*

***persicifolia* 'Cornish Mist'** A delicate-looking plant with soft misty-blue flowers on slender stems above a rosette of shiny, long, deep-green leaves. June to August. **H × S** 90cm × 60cm

punctata* f. *rubriflora Long, puffy, purple-pink flowers cluster thickly along slender, dark red stems above a slowly creeping carpet of mid-green leaves. June to August. **H × S** 60cm × 90cm

'Sarastro' A bushy plant with elongated, tubular, violet-blue bells hanging from leafy, short stems above long, matt-green leaves. Forms a dense, upright clump. June to August. **H × S** 60cm × 60cm

'Swannables' A long-flowering variety that forms a low, rather sprawling clump covered with dangling sprays of smallish lilac bells. July to September. **H × S** 60cm × 60cm

***takesimana* 'Elizabeth'** Short and spreading, its slender stems of long, maroon bells have paler interiors, attractively spotted with soft maroon. June to August. **H × S** 45cm × 60cm. AGM

***trachelium* 'Bernice'** (Nettle-leaved bellflower) The papery, double, deep-violet pixie-hat flowers curl back prettily at the edges. They are carried on slender, upright stems with mid-green, saw-edged leaves. June to August. **H × S** 90cm × 60cm

Campanula persicifolia 'Cornish Mist'

Campanula 'Sarastro'

Campanula punctata f. *rubriflora*

Campanula 'Swannables'

Campanula takesimana 'Elizabeth'

Campanula trachelium 'Bernice'

Catanache caerulea

Centaurea dealbata 'Steenbergii'

Centaurea 'John Coutts'

Centaurea 'Jordy'

Centaurea macrocephala

Centaurea montana

CATANANCHE (Cupid's dart)

caerulea A quick-growing perennial that forms an open clump with wiry stems of flat, semi-double, lavender-blue flowers. The slender petals are fringed at the top and papery. At the base are thin, grass-like leaves. June to September. H × S 60cm × 45cm

Needs Well-drained soil in sun
Great for Front of a border
Bees & Butterflies Yes
For Cutting Yes
Care Can be short-lived, especially in soil that stays wet during winter

CENTAUREA (Knapweed)

These free-flowering, clump-forming plants can be divided into two groups: tall and upright with large, knob-like flowers or short and mounding with flat, wheel-like flowers. In my garden the shorter types form the backbone of the mid-spring border. All have flowers that emerge from a distinctive boss of scaly, papery bracts, and the foliage is also very handsome.

Needs Well-drained soil that does not dry out, in sun or partial shade
Great for Front or back of the border
Bees & Butterflies Yes
For Cutting Yes
Care Remove the old stems and leaves to encourage new flowers and discourage the plant from seeding

dealbata 'Steenbergii' Large, deep-pink to magenta flowers sit on stiff stems with deeply divided, mid-green leaves. It forms a thick, upright clump. The roots are liable to run. June to August. H × S 60cm × 60cm

'John Coutts' A variety with large, soft-mauve flowers and deeply lobed, mid-green leaves, that are white beneath. It forms a broad, mounding clump. May to July. H × S 60cm × 60cm

'Jordy' The most gloriously coloured of all knapweeds with deep-burgundy flowers set off by grey-green leaves. It can get rather leggy, so cut back after flowering. May to August. H × S 60cm × 45cm

macrocephala A sturdy, upright plant with thick, leafy stems topped by large, deep-yellow, thistle-like flowers. The long, pointed, bright-green leaves in alternate pairs form a beautifully sculpted clump, even before the flowers open. June to September. H × S 90cm × 75cm

montana A tough, mound-forming plant with violet-blue flowers carried on short stems, and broad, long silvery leaves. May to September. H × S 45cm × 60cm *montana* **'Alba'** Less vigorous than the blue form, this has pure-white flowers and silver leaves. Planted at the front of a border, it creates an attractive, wide clump. May to June. **H × S** 45cm × 60cm

montana **'Parham'** More upright than other *C. montana* types, this carries its large, rich-lilac flowers on silver stems with silver leaves. May to June. **H × S** 60cm × 45cm

montana **'Purple Heart'** Given the right conditions, this is a vigorous, spreading plant. It produces purple-centred, pure-white flowers and silver leaves. May to June. **H × S** 45cm × 75cm

CENTRANTHUS (Red valerian)

Often seen growing wild in southern counties of the UK, this familiar perennial bears tiny flowers in foamy clusters on short branches with long, waxy, mid- to grey-green leaves. The flowers, which are carried all the way down the flower stems, are followed by fluffy white seeds.

Needs Very well-drained soil, including poor, either clay or sandy, in sun
Great for Middle of a border
Bees & Butterflies Bees
For Cutting Yes
Care Cut back the flower stems as soon as the plant begins to set seed if you don't want it to colonise the garden

ruber Grown from seed, as is the white form (below), this makes an upright, bushy plant with pinkish-red flowers and mid- to grey-green leaves. June to September. **H × S** 75cm × 45cm

ruber **'Albus'** A neat, clean plant with fluffy heads of tiny white flowers and grey-green stems and leaves. June to September. **H × S** 75cm × 45cm

CEPHALARIA (Scabious)

gigantea As the name *gigantea* suggests, this impressive plant needs a good deal of room. It produces large, soft-yellow scabious-like flowers on tall, widely branched stems that rise from a large clump of mid-green leaves. A great choice for a see-through effect in a big border. June to September. **H × S** 180cm × 60cm

Needs Well-drained soil in sun or partial shade
Great for Back of the border
Bees & Butterflies Yes
For Cutting Yes
Care Trouble free

Centaurea montana 'Alba'

Centaurea montana 'Parham'

Centaurea montana 'Purple Heart'

Centranthus ruber

Centranthus ruber 'Albus'

Cephalaria gigantea

Chaerophyllum hirsutum 'Roseum'

Chelone obliqua

Chrysanthemum 'Clara Curtis'

Chrysanthemum 'Mary Stoker'

CHAEROPHYLLUM (Chervil)

hirsutum **'Roseum'** A delightful plant that looks rather like a pink version of our native cow parsley. The flat heads of tiny, soft-pink flowers are carried on thick stems above a lush, broad mound of lacy, soft-green leaves. May to June. **H × S** 90cm × 90cm

Needs Well-drained soil that remains moist in sun or partial shade
Great for Middle of the border
Bees & Butterflies Bees
For Cutting Yes
Care Wild rabbits love this plant so take precautions (*see* p. 33)

CHELONE (Turtlehead)

obliqua Forming a leafy, well behaved, and upright clump, this plant is named for its distinctive blooms, each shaped like the head of a turtle. Short spikes of flowers open towards the top of the rigid stems, clustered four to each side above oval, pointed, dark green leaves. The flowers of the white form, *Chelone glabra*, are a rather dirty shade of white. June to July. **H × S** 90cm × 75cm

Needs Well-drained soil that remains moist in sun or partial shade
Great for Middle of the border
Bees & Butterflies Bees
For Cutting No
Care May take a while to establish, but otherwise trouble free

CHRYSANTHEMUM

Once very popular with cottage gardeners, especially for cutting , the late-flowering hardy chrysanthemums are an absolute delight on dull autumn days. More subtle than the exhibition varieties, these produce sprays of smaller, daisy flowers with slim petals carried on stiff stems with deeply cut leaves. They form soft, mounding clumps.

Needs Well-drained soil in sun
Great for Middle of borders
Bees & Butterflies Yes
For Cutting Yes
Care Trouble free

'Clara Curtis' This pretty plant produces sprays of single, pure-pink flowers with yellow centres that cascade over a broad mound of leaves. September to November. **H × S** 75cm × 75cm

'Mary Stoker' Sprays of single, soft apricot-yellow blooms cover a dense mound of leaves. September to November. **H × S** 75cm × 75cm

CIRSIUM

***rivulare* 'Atropurpureum'** Few perennials can match this for colour. The deep-burgundy, thistle-like flowers, which open just one at a time, are carried in clusters on tall, stiff stems that branch towards the top. At the base is a bushy clump of long, mid-green, rather prickly leaves. June to September. **H × S** 120cm × 50cm

Needs Well-drained soil in sun or partial shade
Great for Middle of the border
Bees & Butterflies Yes
For Cutting No
Care Cut back before the flowers set seed

COREOPSIS (Tickseed)

The yellow forms of this ever-expanding group of plants are the most reliable and bear masses of starry flowers. The stems are wiry and the leaves slim, almost linear. Some varieties are more upright than others.

Needs Well-drained soil in sun
Great for Front of the border
Bees & Butterflies Yes
For Cutting Yes
Care Foliage doesn't emerge until late spring and plants take a while to establish

verticillata Bright-yellow flowers and slender, mid-green leaves adorn this upright form. June to September. **H × S** 45cm × 60cm

***verticillata* 'Moonbeam'** Soft-lemon flowers on wiry stems with bronze-tinted, green leaves form a misty dome. June to September. **H × S** 45cm × 60cm

***verticillata* 'Zagreb'** Ideal for smaller plots, this carries a mass of bright-yellow flowers. June to September. **H × S** 40cm × 45cm. AGM

Cirsium rivulare 'Atropurpureum'

Coreopsis verticillata

Coreopsis verticillata 'Moonbeam'

Coreopsis verticillata 'Zagreb'

Crocosmia × crocosmiiflora 'Emily McKenzie'

Crocosmia × crocosmiiflora 'Solfatare'

CROCOSMIA (Montbretia)

Indispensable for their warm, late-summer colours, crocosmias carry sprays of small, lily-like flowers on stems that arch over clumps of grassy, mid-green leaves. Red varieties tend to be hardier than yellow ones.

Needs Well-drained soil in sun
Great for Middle of the border
Bees & Butterflies No
For Cutting Yes
Care Trouble free. Yellow varieties can be less hardy in wet ground

× *crocosmiiflora* 'Emily McKenzie' Adds a bold splash of rich orange to any border. July to September. **H × S** 60cm × 50cm. AGM

× *crocosmiiflora* 'George Davison' A tough, bushy plant with sprays of small, soft apricot-yellow flowers and mid-green leaves. July to September. **H × S** 75cm × 60cm

× *crocosmiiflora* 'Solfatare' Flowers of soft yellow face outwards and the leaves are tinted with bronze. July to September. **H × S** 60cm × 50cm. AGM

'Emberglow' A neat plant with small red flowers and pleated, mid-green leaves. July to September. **H × S** 90cm × 75cm

'Lucifer' Adding drama to any border, the brilliant red flowers are upward-facing and its sword-like leaves are pleated. July to September. **H × S** 90cm × 75cm. AGM

'Okavango' Displaying a fruity mix of vibrant orange overlaid with pink, the flowers form neat 'V'-shaped sprays. July to September. **H × S** 75cm × 60cm

'Paul's Best Yellow' A good yellow variety with large, bright, outward-facing flowers. July to September. **H × S** 90cm × 60cm

Crocosmia × crocosmiiflora 'George Davison'

Crocosmia 'Emberglow'

Crocosmia 'Lucifer'

Crocosmia 'Okavango'

Crocosmia 'Paul's Best Yellow'

DELPHINIUM

These stalwarts of the grand herbaceous border offer structure and well-defined height. Although there are many named varieties, most are expensive and difficult to obtain. The varieties described here are raised from seed selected from the Pacific Hybrids Series of plants. They were raised decades ago in the USA, so colours may vary slightly. All bear flower spikes packed with disc-like blooms, which have buff or black centres known as 'bees' or 'eyes'. The spikes tower above a mounding clump of delicately fingered, mid-green leaves.

Needs Well-drained soil in sun
Great for Back of the border
Bees & Butterflies Bees
For Cutting Yes
Care Give plants rich, deep, well-dug soil and add manure to get the best results. Protect from slugs

'Astolat' A variety with spikes of semi-double, soft lilac-pink blooms with buff or black 'bees'. June to July. **H × S** 180cm × 90cm

'Black Knight' The single, dark blue flowers of this elegant plant have centres that are generally black, but sometimes white. June to July. **H × S** 180cm × 90cm

'Blue Bird' A good mixer that bears semi-double, mid-blue flowers with white centres. June to July. **H × S** 180cm × 90cm

'Galahad' A white-flowered, semi-double form with contrasting black centres. June to July. **H × S** 180cm × 90cm

'Summer Skies' Lovely soft-blue, semi-double flowers with white eyes. June to July. **H × S** 180cm × 90cm

Delphinium 'Astolat'

Delphinium 'Black Knight'

Delphinium 'Galahad'

Delphinium 'Summer Skies'

Delphinium 'Blue Bird'

Dianthus cruentus

Dianthus 'Devon Wizard'

Dianthus 'Mrs Sinkins'

Dicentra formosa

Dicentra 'King of Hearts'

DIANTHUS (Pink)

There are hundreds of different pinks. Most fall into the category of border pinks and many have fragrant flowers that are good for cutting. Yet many are not exactly elegant and few make great garden plants. I have chosen three of my favourites and all fit well into a border.

Needs Well-drained soil in sun
Great for Front of the border
Bees & Butterflies Bees
For Cutting Yes
Care Trim back in spring to neaten untidy clumps of leaves. Poisonous if eaten.

cruentus (Blood pink) An elegant little plant with clusters of small, single, rich-red flowers popping out of tightly packed, dark maroon calyces. Carried on tall stems high above a clump of short, spiky leaves, they create an attractive wispy effect. June to August.
H × S 70cm × 30cm

'Devon Wizard' A free-flowering plant with lots of neatly shaped, carmine-pink flowers borne on slender stems above a bushy clump of evergreen, grey leaves. June to September. **H × S** 30cm × 45cm. AGM

'Mrs Sinkins' This classic pink produces large, shaggy, heavily scented, white flowers from a rather sprawling clump of evergreen, mid-green leaves. June to August **H × S** 30cm × 30cm

DICENTRA (Bleeding heart)

Although these plants are truly delightful, they can be really fussy about where they choose to grow. The two included here perform well in a border. The flowers look like puffy hearts and are carried on brittle stems just above a slowly spreading mound of lush, almost succulent-looking, lacy leaves. (For *Dicentra spectabilis* see *Lamprocapnos spectabilis* on p. 123.)

Needs Cool, humus-rich soil that remains moist in partial or full shade
Great for Shady areas such as woodland
Bees & Butterflies No
For Cutting No
Care Trouble free in the right spot

formosa A low, spreading plant with small sprays of slender, locket-shaped, soft-pink flowers on arching stems above deeply divided, fresh-green leaves. May to June.
H × S 45cm × 45cm

'King of Hearts' This is an incredibly long-flowering plant with small clusters of perfect heart-shaped, rich-pink flowers on slender stems above a spreading mound of handsome, lacy, grey-green leaves. May to October. **H × S** 30cm × 45cm

DICTAMNUS (Burning bush)

albus Patience is required to grow this delicate plant, which can be very slow to germinate. The white flowers, which resemble butterflies, have maroon-veined, widely spaced petals and long, curling stamens. They are carried in open spires up sticky, red-tinged stems with thick, shiny, mid-green leaves. Most plants are raised from seed, so may be variable in colour. *D. albus* var. *purpureus* is similar, but the large-veined magenta flowers fade to pink. July to August. **H × S** 90cm × 75cm. AGM

Needs Well-drained soil in sun or partial shade
Great for Middle of the border
Bees & Butterflies No
For Cutting No
Care Trouble free, but slow to establish

DIGITALIS (Foxglove)

Elegant and very upright, these glorious plants add gracefulness to a border with their spires of long, tubular flowers arising from an evergreen rosette of leaves. Many are biennial and die after flowering; those listed here are perennial, but short-lived.

Needs Well-drained soil in sun or shade
Great for Middle of a border
Bees & Butterflies Bees
For Cutting Yes
Care Can be short-lived, so allow the plants to seed

ferruginea The small, honey-coloured flowers, veined inside with brown, are subtle and stylish. They are borne above a rosette of evergreen, shiny, dark green leaves. June to September. **H × S** 90cm × 30cm. AGM

'Glory of Roundway' This lovely plant has slim spikes of long, slender, soft apricot-pink flowers and a thick rosette of dark green leaves. Sadly, it does not set seed. June to August. **H × S** 75cm × 30cm

grandiflora The large, pale-yellow flowers and soft-green leaves create a pretty effect. June to July. **H × S** 75cm × 30cm. AGM

lutea Slender spikes of small, pale-lemon flowers are displayed above long, shiny deep-green leaves. June to September. **H × S** 90cm × 30cm

× *mertonensis* Stumpy spikes covered with dusky-pink flowers adorn this variety, which can be temperamental. July to August. **H × S** 75cm × 30cm. AGM

Dictamnus albus

Digitalis ferruginea

Digitalis 'Glory of Roundway'

Digitalis grandiflora

Digitalis lutea

Digitalis × mertonensis

Echinacea 'Green Envy'

Echinacea 'Harvest Moon'

Echinacea 'Marmalade'

Echinacea pallida

Echinacea purpurea

Echincea purpurea 'Coconut Lime'

ECHINACEA (Coneflower)

The spiky centres of these striking daisies start out flat then, as the flower ages, they increase in size to form a tall, often pointed, cone. Carried on stiff, upright stems, in some varieties they are scented, and all are held above oval, pointed, mid-green leaves. In North America, where they grow wild, flower colours tend to be pinks or yellows. In recent years, however, there has been an eruption of new varieties, extending the colour range to include orange and green. Some do not thrive in our wet climate.

Needs Well-drained soil in sun
Great for Middle of the border
Bees & Butterflies Yes
For Cutting Yes
Care Coneflowers are gaining a reputation for being short-lived and they can be tricky to keep going. I cut off the seedheads as soon as possible

'Green Envy' An unusual colour for flowers, the green of this variety is heavily stained with magenta. There are big gaps between the petals and the central disc is brown. July to September. **H × S** 90cm × 50cm

'Harvest Moon' The flowers have slender, relaxed, deep-yellow petals that harmonise with the bronze central cone. July to September. **H × S** 75cm × 50cm

'Marmalade' An orange flower with a centre of shorter, fringed petals that gives the bloom a distinctive shaggy look. July to September. **H × S** 75cm × 50cm

pallida Soft-magenta flowers, their petals drooping around the tightly domed centres, are carried on slender stems. Needs a dry soil. July to August. **H × S** 105cm × 50cm

purpurea The parent of many varieties. Bears large, single, purplish-pink flowers, each with a flat bronze-brown centre that grows into a handsome cone. July to September. **H × S** 90cm × 60cm. AGM

purpurea 'Coconut Lime' A large central disc of short, lime-green spikes – bronze in the middle – is surrounded by white petals. July to September. **H × S** 75cm × 50cm

purpurea 'Green Jewel' A variety with frilly, lime-green flowers and a prominent green centre. July to September. **H × S** 75cm × 50cm

purpurea 'Hope' A lovely plant with soft-magenta flowers. The large, flat centre rises up to form a broad dome. July to September. **H × S** 75cm × 50cm

purpurea 'Magnus' An award-winner with large, fragrant, reddish-pink flowers. Usually raised from seed so may be variable. July to September. **H × S** 90cm × 60cm. AGM *purpurea* **'White Swan'** Surrounded by white petals, the large, greenish cones of this variety turn bronze. Usually seed-raised. July to September. **H × S** 90cm × 60cm

'Sundown' A fragrant, orange-red flowered coneflower. The blooms take on shades of pink as they mature. July to September. **H × S** 90cm × 50cm

'Sunrise' The glossy, rich-yellow flowers of this fragrant variety have pink undersides and their green centres turn copper with age. July to September. **H × S** 90cm × 50cm

'Tomato Soup' Vivid orange-scarlet flowers become more orange as they fade. July to September. **H × S** 75cm × 50cm

Echinacea purpurea 'Green Jewel'

Echincea purpurea 'Hope'

Echincea purpurea 'Magnus'

Echincea purpurea 'White Swan'

Echinacea 'Sundown'

Echinacea 'Sunrise'

Echinacea 'Tomato Soup'

Echinops bannaticus 'Blue Globe' and *Monarda* 'Scorpion' with *Echinacea purpurea* (foreground)

ECHINOPS (Globe thistle)

Loved by butterflies and bees, the flowers of these sculptural plants are intriguing. The small florets are packed so closely together they form a tight, perfectly round ball that is spiky when in bud. As the flowers open into little stars, the ball softens into a fuzzy sphere. They are carried on tall, rigid, usually silver stems, above a clump of long, mid-green, deeply divided leaves with silver undersides. Drought tolerant, they will grow in a wide range of soils.

Needs Well-drained soil in sun or partial shade
Great for Middle or back of the border
Bees & Butterflies Bees
For Cutting Yes
Care Trouble free

bannaticus **'Blue Globe'** A seed-raised plant with lots of big, violet-blue flowers and mid-green leaves. June to August. **H × S** 120cm × 90cm

bannaticus **'Taplow Blue'** Pale-blue flowers are carried on mid-green stems above silver-green leaves. An easy variety to grow. July to September. **H × S** 120cm × 90cm

ritro A robust plant with small, silver-blue flowers carried on stiff, mid-green stems. July to September. **H × S** 90cm × 60cm. AGM

ritro **'Veitch's Blue'** Small, rich-blue spheres are borne on silver stems above silver leaves. July to September. **H × S** 90cm × 50cm

sphaerocephalus **'Arctic Glow'** Luminous grey-white flowers bloom on pale-mauve stems. Although short-lived, the plant comes true from seed and thrives in sandy soils. July to August. **H × S** 90cm × 50cm

Echinops bannaticus 'Blue Globe'

Echinops bannaticus 'Taplow Blue'

Echinops ritro

Echinops ritro 'Veitch's Blue'

Echinops sphaerocephalus 'Arctic Glow'

Epimedium 'Amber Queen'

Epimedium × rubrum

Epimedium × cantabrigiense

Epimedium × versicolor 'Cupreum'

EPIMEDIUM (Barrenwort)

Demure yet very hardy, these shade-loving plants are covered with sprays of small (sometimes tiny), cap-shaped flowers during spring. The flowers are held daintily on wiry stems and dance above a mound of often papery, sometimes leathery, heart-shaped leaves. Many are evergreen and some turn gorgeous colours in autumn.

Needs Well-drained soil with leaf mould, in partial shade or full shade. *E. × versicolor* varieties cope with dry soils
Great for Shade near or beneath shrubs and trees
Bees & Butterflies Bees
For Cutting No
Care Most will take a little time to establish, otherwise trouble free

'Amber Queen' Long, airy sprays of small, copper-yellow flowers with long, curved spurs are carried above evergreen, deep-green leaves that are serrated at the edges. April to June, and often in September. **H × S** 45cm × 60cm

× *cantabrigiense* A distinctly wispy plant that comes into its own when it blooms in spring. Long sprays of tiny, cupped, cream and pink-red flowers hover above a mound of evergreen, leathery leaves. April to June. **H × S** 45cm × 60cm

× *rubrum* An easy variety to grow with large, yet delicate, bright-red flowers displaying white centres. The thick leaves are richly tinted with red in spring. April to May. **H × S** 30cm × 45cm. AGM

Epimedium × versicolor 'Sulphureum'

Epimedium × warleyense 'Orangekönigin'

Epimedium × youngianum 'Niveum'

× *versicolor* 'Cupreum' Soft pink-red flowers with pale-yellow centres are carried in dense sprays above evergreen, lime-green leaves that turn orange-red in autumn. April to June. **H × S** 45cm × 60cm

× *versicolor* 'Sulphureum' A free-flowering plant with sprays of pale-yellow and white flowers. These are carried just above evergreen, deep-green leaves handsomely burnished with red from autumn to spring. April to May. **H × S** 45cm × 75cm. AGM

× *warleyense* 'Orangekönigin' Produces open sprays of delicate, peach-orange flowers with tight, yellow centres. They seem to flutter above the evergreen leaves, which are heavily tinged with red in winter. April to June. **H × S** 45cm × 60cm

× *youngianum* 'Niveum' A charming plant with small, white flowers carried on reddish stems above a neat mound of leaves. These are coppery at first. April to May. **H × S** 30cm × 45cm. AGM

ERIGERON (Fleabane)

Simple and delightful, these small, slim-petalled daisies sit well next to most perennials. The flowers are produced in great quantities above a low, spreading clump of mid-green leaves.

Needs Well-drained soil in sun or partial shade
Great for Front of the border
Bees & Butterflies Yes
For Cutting Yes
Care Rabbits love them, especially the larger types, otherwise trouble free

'Dignity' A dark-flowered variety with small sprays of single, rich-violet flowers above a mound of mid-green leaves. June to August. **H × S** 45cm × 60cm

'Dunkelste Aller' A free-flowering plant with semi-double, violet flowers carried on short stems above mid-green leaves. June to August. **H × S** 45cm × 60cm

karvinskianus This prostrate plant is littered with little daisies for months. Each bloom opens pink, slowly turning to white and creating a two-tone effect. Good in pots and in walls, it will seed around when happy. June to August. **H × S** 15cm × 60cm. AGM

'Rosa Juwel' Soft lilac-pink flowers are carried on upright stems above a mat of mid-green leaves. June to August. **H × S** 45cm × 60cm

'Schneewittchen' Charming white, semi-double flowers become tinged with palest pink as they age. On a raised edge, it will create a waterfall of pure white over time. June to August. **H × S** 45cm × 60cm

Erigeron 'Dignity'

Erigeron 'Dunkelste Aller'

Erigeron karvinskianus

Erigeron 'Rosa Juwel'

Erigeron 'Schneewittchen'

Erodium manescavii

Eryngium alpinum

Eryngium bourgatii

Eryngium planum

ERODIUM (Heron's bill)

manescavii This plant resembles a hardy geranium and in many ways behaves like one. The open pink flowers are carried on straight stems that shoot like sparklers from a crown of deeply divided, mid-green leaves. The seedheads are spear-like. June to September. **H × S** 45cm × 45cm

Needs Well-drained soil in sun
Great for Front of the border
Bees & Butterflies Yes
For Cutting No
Care Trouble free

ERYNGIUM (Sea holly)

The flowers of these architectural plants bring an abstract quality to a border. Cone-shaped and surrounded by spiky collars, they are borne on stiff stems above a clump or rosette of evergreen leaves.

Needs Well-drained soil, including very dry and clay soils, in sun
Great for Front or middle of the border
Bees & Butterflies Yes
For Cutting Yes
Care Dislikes waterlogged soils; perfect for coastal and gravel gardens

alpinum An extremely beautiful plant with towering soft-green cones that turn steely- blue. These are encased within a lacy upturned ruff with short, spiky edges. The shiny leaves are bright green. July to August. **H × S** 75cm × 45cm

bourgatii Stiffly upright, the blue, well-branched stems are topped by small, mid-blue flowers with prickly, blue collars. The leaves are dark green. July to September. **H × S** 60cm × 45cm

Eryngium × *tripartitum*

Eryngium variifolium

Eryngium × *zabelii* 'Big Blue'

planum A network of slender blue stems carries little, light-blue flowers above a rosette of spatula-shaped, deep-green leaves. Usually seed grown, so variable. July to August. **H × S** 90cm × 45cm

× *tripartitum* A free-flowering plant with small, light-blue flowers and slim, short spikes that deepen to violet-blue. At the base sits a rosette of dark green leaves. July to August. **H × S** 60cm × 30cm. AGM

variifolium Small white flowers, arranged up stout, soft-maroon stems, turn blue with age. The spiky, green leaves display white marbling and form a flat rosette. July to August. **H × S** 45cm × 30cm

× *zabelii* 'Big Blue' The strikingly shaped flowers with large, ink-blue, starry collars are attractive to bees. They are carried on well-branched stems above divided, mid-green leaves. July to August. **H × S** 60cm × 30cm

EUPATORIUM (Joe Pye weed)

Initially unremarkable, by midsummer and right through to late autumn, this large plant evolves into a truly handsome upright clump. The stems are usually dark red with whorls of long, deep-green, pointed leaves carried right to the top. Broad, domed heads of little flowers pale in colour as they age and become fluffy. They make a wonderful larder for all insects.

Needs Well-drained soil that remains moist in sun or partial shade.
Great for Back of the border
Bees & Butterflies Yes
For Cutting Yes
Care Trouble free in heavy soils and those that don't dry out. Usually needs no staking

dubium **'Little Joe'** Most eupatoriums are large. This shorter variety has rosy-purple flowers on purple stems with deep-green, oval leaves. August to September. **H × S** 105cm × 75cm

maculatum **'Riesenschirm'** A majestic plant. Large, domed, dusky-pink heads are carried on dark maroon stems. August to September. **H × S** 180cm × 90cm. AGM

purpureum Loosely domed heads of purple-pink flowers on upright red stems with whorls of pointed, mid-green leaves. August to September. **H × S** 180cm × 90cm

Eupatorium dubium 'Little Joe'

Eupatorium maculatum 'Riesenschirm'

Eupatorium purpureum

Euphorbia amygdaloides 'Purpurea'

Euphorbia amygdaloides var. *robbiae*

Euphorbia dulcis 'Chameleon'

Euphorbia griffithii 'Fireglow'

Euphorbia myrsinites

Euphorbia wallichii

EUPHORBIA (Spurge)

Perfect for creating year-round structure, most euphorbias have evergreen leaves, which make whorls around the stiff stems, and grow into neat, leafy mounds. In spring these are topped with clusters or spires of small flowers that are almost hidden by large, colourful bracts.

Needs Well-drained soil in sun or partial shade; some varieties prefer shade
Great for Front or middle of the border
Bees & Butterflies No
For Cutting No
Care These plants can take a while to mature, so make sure you leave enough space around them. Also, wear gloves when handling – some people are allergic to the milky sap that seeps out of broken stems

***amygdaloides* 'Purpurea'** (Wood spurge) Broad, towering spikes of lime-green flowers are carried above a dense mound of evergreen, dark green leaves heavily tinged with maroon. A woodlander that is ideal for a semi-shady spot. April to June. **H × S** 60cm × 60cm

amygdaloides* var. *robbiae A useful evergreen plant with whorls of leathery, dark green leaves. The stems are topped with tall spikes of yellow-green flowers. Great for a dry, shady spot, where it will spread slowly. April to June. **H × S** 60cm × 90cm. AGM

***dulcis* 'Chameleon'** Long, rich-mahogany leaves unfurl in spring to form an airy mound, which carries sprays of lime-green flowers. The plant readily self-seeds and can be prone to rust disease, but looks good dotted around a shady border. May to June. **H × S** 30cm × 60cm

***griffithii* 'Fireglow'** A handsome, upright plant that forms broad swathes. Long, red-tinged, mid-green leaves are carried up red stems that are topped with flat clusters of red-orange flowers. In autumn the leaves turn fiery-red for a short time before they fall. May to July. **H × S** 90cm × 75cm

myrsinites The distinctive grey leaves of this evergreen remind me of dinosaur scales. They form whorls around long, prostrate stems that end in flat clusters of lime-green flowers. A short plant for well-drained soils, including poor and dry ones. April to June. **H × S** 15cm × 60cm. AGM

wallichii A very upright, bushy plant. The long, dark green leaves are carried all the way up stems topped with lime-green flowers. May to August. **H × S** 60cm × 45cm

GALIUM (Sweet woodruff)

odoratum In spring, the flowers of this charming perennial resemble clusters of tiny, white stars. Faintly scented, they are carried on slender stems ringed by narrow, bright green leaves. These create a short, lush, slowly spreading carpet – the perfect ground-cover for shady areas. April to May. **H × S** 30cm × 60cm

Needs Well-drained soil in partial shade
Great for Shade, especially among shrubs and trees
Bees & Butterflies No
For Cutting No
Care Trouble free

GERANIUM (Hardy geranium)

Perhaps the most versatile perennials, hardy geraniums blend effortlessly into a border and, with hundreds of varieties to choose from, there is a plant for every style of garden. The flowers are produced in great quantities and most are carried on long stems just above the lush, deeply divided leaves, which enhance the garden's green tapestry.

Needs Well-drained soil in sun to light shade
Great for Front and middle of the border; a few varieties are fine for the back
Bees & Butterflies Bees
For Cutting No
Care Trouble free. To keep soft-pink flowered varieties in check, dead-head before the seeds are scattered around. Shorter varieties are slower to establish. Cut spent top growth right back to soil level after flowering to encourage further flowers

'Ann Folkard' A low, spreading plant, the black-eyed, deep magenta flowers are carried on long, sprawling stems. The mid-green leaves are yellow when young. May to September. **H × S** 30cm × 75cm. AGM

'Azure Rush' A sport of *G.* 'Rozanne', the flat, soft-blue flowers with white eyes are saucer-shaped. They are carried above a carpet of mid-green, deeply divided leaves. June to October. **H × S** 30cm × 60cm

'Blue Cloud' Impressive for the misty waterfall of shallowly cupped, soft lilac-blue flowers on short, branching stems above deeply divided leaves. May to August. **H × S** 60cm × 75cm. AGM

'Blushing Turtle' Originally called 'Breathless', this oddly named plant flowers continuously for many months. The deep-pink flowers cover a dense dome of mid-green leaves. May to September. **H × S** 30cm × 60cm

Galium odoratum

Geranium 'Ann Folkard'

Geranium 'Azure Rush'

Geranium 'Blushing Turtle'

Geranium 'Blue Cloud'

Geranium 'Brookside'

Geranium clarkei 'Kashmir Pink'

Geranium clarkei 'Kashmir White'

Geranium 'Dragon Heart'

'Brookside' Violet-blue flowers, each with a tiny, white centre, smother a broad clump of divided, mid-green leaves over a long period. June to September. **H × S** 45cm × 60cm. AGM

clarkei **'Kashmir Pink'** One for the front of the border. Pretty, pale-pink flowers are carried in clusters above a mound of deeply divided, mid-green leaves. May to June. **H × S** 45cm × 60cm

clarkei **'Kashmir White'** White geraniums are few. This one has sprays of large, mauve-veined flowers and deeply divided leaves. May to June. **H × S** 45cm × 60cm

'Dragon Heart' Magenta, black-centred flowers, larger than most, are borne on slender stems with deeply cut leaves. A plant that sprawls and weaves its way around others. June to September. **H × S** 45cm × 60cm

'Elke' A neat carpeting plant, perfect for the front of a border, covered with small, deep-pink flowers. Their paler edges and white centres make them stand out. May to August. **H × S** 23cm × 30cm

himalayense **'Derrick Cook'** A great plant for edging a border. It spreads to form a tumbling mound of mid-green leaves covered with masses of large, white, maroon-veined flowers. June to August. **H × S** 45cm × 60cm

himalayense **'Gravetye'** At one time a very popular blue variety, this has largely been superseded by longer-flowering plants. Still worth growing for its spreading foliage that takes on beautiful red tones in autumn. June to August. **H × S** 45cm × 60cm

Geranium 'Elke'

Geranium himalayense 'Derrick Cook'

Geranium himalayense 'Gravetye'

'Johnson's Blue' A classic variety with saucer-shaped, indigo-blue flowers borne above a compact mound of delicate-looking, deeply divided, dark green leaves. May to August. **H × S** 60cm × 60cm

macrorrhizum An excellent hardy geranium for ground-cover in shady, dry spots. The clusters of flat, cerise-pink flowers on longish stems rise above a thick carpet of leaves. These are round, hairy, unusually scented, and semi-evergreen. May to June. **H × S** 45cm × 60cm

macrorrhizum **'Ingwerson's Variety'** Similar to the species, but with flowers of a softer lilac-pink. May to June. **H × S** 45cm × 60cm. AGM

macrorrhizum **'White-Ness'** A dwarf plant that spreads over time to form a ground-covering mat. The clusters of pure white flowers are carried just above small, round, bright-green leaves. May to June. **H × S** 30cm × 45cm. AGM

× *magnificum* Large, flat, rich-blue flowers with purple veins are carried above a vigorous mound of mid-green leaves. For a short time in autumn these turn pure red. June to August. **H × S** 60cm × 60cm. AGM

'Mavis Simpson' A prostrate carpet of small, round, grey-green leaves is covered with neat, open, silvery-pink flowers. Best grown in a very well-drained soil. June to September. **H × S** 23cm × 45cm. AGM

'Nimbus' Incredibly free flowering, this variety sends out sprays of mid-sized, lilac-blue flowers, each with a tiny white centre. They are carried above a pretty mound of finely divided, mid-green leaves. June to September. **H × S** 45cm × 45cm. AGM

Geranium 'Johnson's Blue'

Geranium macrorrhizum

Geranium macrorrhizum 'Ingwerson's Variety'

Geranium macrorrhizum 'White-Ness'

Geraranium × *magnificum*

Geranium 'Mavis Simpson'

Geranium 'Nimbus'

Geranium × *oxonianum* 'Patricia Josephine' (foreground) with *Geranium* 'Orion', *Gillenia trifoliata* and orange *Geum* 'Totally Tangerine'

nodosum The little, lilac-pink, trumpet-shaped flowers are scattered across a dense hummock of divided, glossy foliage. Often grown from seed, the flowers can vary from soft pink to deep lilac. Good for shady areas, even where the soil is fairly dry. June to August. **H × S** 30cm × 60cm

***nodosum* 'Silverwood'** As the name suggests, the flowers of this variety are pure white and combine beautifully with the hummock of divided, glossy foliage. Not widely available but well worth seeking out. June to August. **H × S** 30cm × 60cm

'Orion' A very free-flowering variety that forms a loose, spreading plant. The large, glowing, deep-blue flowers with white centres are carried well above the mound of deeply divided, mid-green leaves. June to September. **H × S** 75cm × 60cm. AGM

× *oxonianum* 'A. T. Johnson' Of all the pink-flowered hardy geraniums, the *G.* × *oxonianum* forms produce the most plentiful flowers. They also freely self seed. This older variety bears great quantities of small, glowing-pink, trumpet-shaped flowers above a mound of divided, mid-green leaves. June to August. **H × S** 40cm × 40cm. AGM

× *oxonianum* 'Lace Time' A plant of soft colours, its small trumpet-shaped flowers are pale pink, while the divided leaves form a pale-green mound. June to August. **H × S** 40cm × 40cm

× *oxonianum* 'Patricia Josephine' I named this lovely plant after my mother. Preferring a more naturalistic style of gardening, she never removed any seedlings and I found this growing in her garden. I consider it one of the best and longest-flowering pink hardy geraniums. From a thick, vigorous mound of foliage, the soft silver-pink, trumpet-shaped flowers just keep on coming, gradually fading to near white. The divided, mid-green leaves have maroon spots on each division. June to August. **H × S** 55cm × 60cm

× *oxonianum* 'Rose Clair' Pretty trumpet-shaped flowers open a shiny, pure pink and become paler, almost white with age. They are carried above an open mound of mid-green leaves. June to August. **H × S** 45cm × 45cm

'Patricia' Abundant sprays of open, cerise-pink flowers rise above a spreading mound of mid-green leaves. The foliage is deeply cut into three sections. June to September. **H × S** 75cm × 90cm. AGM

Geranium nodosum

Geranium nodosum 'Silverwood'

Geranium × *oxonianum* 'A. T. Johnson'

Geranium × *oxonianum* 'Lace Time'

Geranium × *oxonianum* 'Rose Clair'

Geranium 'Patricia'

Geranium phaeum

Geranium phaeum 'Album'

Geranium phaeum 'Raven'

Geranium phaeum var. *phaeum* 'Samobor'

Geranium 'Philippe Vapelle'

Geranium pratense 'Hocus Pocus'

Geranium pratense 'Mrs. Kendall Clark'

Geranium pratense var *pratense* f. *albiflorum*

Geranium renardii

phaeum (Mourning widow) Ideal for a shady spot that does not dry out. The flat, slightly ruffled, dark burgundy flowers display long stamens that poke out from the centre. They sit in clusters on tall stems above deeply divided, dark maroon-spotted leaves. May to June. **H × S** 90cm × 60cm

phaeum **'Album'** Excellent for brightening up shady areas, this variety bears almost translucent white flowers in loose sprays. The upright stems have mid-green leaves. May to June. **H × S** 75cm × 45cm

phaeum **'Raven'** Named for its flat, darkest-purple flowers borne on tall stems above a mound of divided, bright-green leaves. May to June. **H × S** 75cm × 45cm

phaeum **var.** *phaeum* **'Samobor'** The flowers are dark burgundy, like those of *G. phaeum*, but the foliage is distinctive. Worth growing for its mound of mid-green leaves decorated with a broad ring of maroon. May to June. **H × S** 90cm × 60cm

'Philippe Vapelle' Not the longest-flowering variety but once the large, pale-violet flowers are over, the tight mound of velvety, grey-green leaves remains particularly attractive. June to July. **H × S** 30cm × 30cm

pratense **'Hocus Pocus'** Unusual foliage colour marks out this variety. Clusters of large, mid-blue flowers sit above a mound of almost black, deeply divided leaves. Works well in a pot. May to July. **H × S** 30cm × 30cm

pratense **'Mrs Kendall Clark'** (Meadow cranesbill) The pale-blue flowers are veined with white and carried in clusters above deeply divided, mid-green leaves. May to July. **H × S** 90cm × 45cm. AGM

pratense **var.** *pratense* **f.** *albiflorum* (Meadow cranesbill) A tall plant with sprays of open white flowers carried on branched stems above deeply divided, soft green leaves. Often grown from seed, sometimes the stamens can be black, or the petals tinged with soft blue. May to July. **H × S** 90cm × 45cm

psilostemon The tallest hardy geranium with masses of black-eyed, vivid magenta flowers. These are held in sprays on slender stems well above a mound of deeply divided, mid-green leaves. Best grown towards the back of the border. June to August. **H × S** 105cm × 90cm. AGM

renardii A lovely plant with a soft mound of round, notched, velvety, sage-green leaves. Clusters of open, purple-veined, white flowers are held just above the foliage. May to June. **H × S** 30cm × 30cm. AGM

Geranium psilostemon in our garden will tumble forwards over other plants if not cut back

× *riversleaianum* 'Russell Prichard' This prostrate, slowly spreading plant has deep cerise-pink flowers and silver-grey leaves. More reliable grown in very free-draining soil. June to July. **H × S** 23cm × 45cm. AGM

'Rozanne' A much applauded, free-flowering plant with large, blue, white-centred flowers carried for many months just above a spreading clump of deeply divided leaves. May to September. **H × S** 60cm × 75cm. AGM

***sanguineum* 'Album'** (Bloody cranesbill) An ideal variety for the front of the border where its delicate white flowers can be appreciated. They cover a low dome of small, mid-green leaves. June to July. **H × S** 23cm × 60cm. AGM

***sanguineum* 'Max Frei'** A carpeting plant with divided, mid-green leaves. The large flowers are a vivid shade of magenta. June to July. **H × S** 23cm × 45cm

sanguineum* var. *striatum Open, soft-pink flowers stand up over a carpet of deeply fingered, mid-green leaves. June to August. **H × S** 23cm × 45cm. AGM

'Sirak' Blooming over a long period, the clusters of large, lilac flowers rise above a neat mound of soft grey-green leaves. June to August. **H × S** 45cm × 45cm. AGM

'Stephanie' Early to flower, sending up sprays of large, open, lilac flowers, veined with purple. The soft, round, mid-green leaves form a dense broad clump. May to June. **H × S** 50cm × 60cm

'Sweet Heidy' A spreading plant with large, saucer-shaped, lilac-blue flowers displaying hints of pink and white in the centre. June to September. **H × S** 35cm × 45cm

***sylvaticum* 'Album'** (Wood cranesbill) Bright-white flowers are carried in sprays on tall, branched stems above deeply divided, bright-green leaves. Great for shadier spots. May to June. **H × S** 75cm × 45cm. AGM

***sylvaticum* 'Mayflower'** Sprays of glowing, violet-blue flowers on upright, branched stems sit above divided, bright green leaves. May to June. **H × S** 75cm × 45cm. AGM

***wallichianum* 'Crystal Lake'** An impressive sprawling, free-flowering plant. Medium-sized, soft lilac-blue flowers with dark purple veins are carried in ones and twos above deeply divided, mid-green leaves. May to October. **H × S** 45cm × 60cm

wlassovianum The last of the geraniums to bloom. Small, open, dark violet flowers on arching stems emerge from a mound of dark green leaves that turn briefly red in autumn. July to September. **H × S** 60cm × 75cm

Geranium 'Rozanne' with *Lysimachia punctata* 'Alexander'

Geranium × *riversleaianum* 'Russell Prichard'

Geranium sanguineum 'Album'

Geranium sanguineum 'Max Frei'

Geranium sanguineum var. striatum

Geranium 'Sirak'

Geranium 'Stephanie'

Geranium 'Sweet Heidy'

Geranium sylvaticum 'Album'

Geranium sylvaticum 'Mayflower'

Geranium wallichianum 'Crystal Lake'

Geranium wlassovianum

Geum 'Bell Bank'

Geum 'Borisii'

Geum 'Flames of Passion'

Geum 'Georgenberg'

Geum 'Lady Stratheden'

Geum 'Lemon Drops'

GEUM (Avens)

This group of eye-catching plants includes spring-flowering varieties and others that bloom from early summer right through to mid-autumn. The flowers are often brightly coloured and single or semi-double; some open flat, while others are bell shaped. They are carried on branched stems above a carpet or mound of hairy leaves.

Needs Well-drained soil that remains moist in sun or partial shade
Great for Front of a border, but can be grown in containers
Bees & Butterflies Bees
For Cutting Yes, but only the tall varieties
Care If the short varieties dry out they are easily revived with water

'Bell Bank' Slender stems of nodding, semi-double, reddish-pink flowers bloom for many weeks above a dense, spreading clump of mid-green leaves. May to July. H × S 30cm × 45cm

'Borisii' The upward-facing, single, deep-orange flowers are held individually above a low, neat mound of mid-green leaves. The first flush is followed by occasional blooms through until autumn. May to September. H × S 30cm × 30cm

'Flames of Passion' Handsome and free-flowering, the semi-double flowers of this variety open red and fade with age to tones of orange. The blooms dangle from tall stems above a dense mound of leaves. May to July. H × S 45cm × 45cm

'Georgenberg' A carpeting plant with a slowly spreading mound of mid-green leaves. The short stems of upward-facing, single flowers are a bright yet deep yellow. May to September. H × S 30cm × 30cm

'Lady Stratheden' Well-known and popular, this variety blooms for many weeks and the cut flowers last well in water. Tall, branched stems of semi-double, rich-yellow flowers are held high above a clump of mid-green leaves. Comes true when raised from seed. May to September. H × S 60cm × 50cm. AGM

'Lemon Drops' A delightful plant with many small, bell-shaped, lemon flowers on branched bronzed stems just above a broad, spreading mound of leaves. May to June. H × S 30cm × 45cm

'Mai Tai' A recently introduced free-flowering variety, part of the 'Cocktail' series. The large, frilly, semi-double, apricot-peach flowers sit above a wide mound of mid-green leaves, softening in colour as they age. May to July. H × S 45cm × 45cm

'Marmalade' Similar in form to 'Lemon Drops', but with tangerine-orange, bell-shaped flowers opening from dark buds. These dangle from reddish, branched stems above a mound of mid-green leaves. May to June. **H × S** 30cm × 45cm

'Mrs J. Bradshaw' The large, semi-double, scarlet flowers are carried on tall, upright, branched stems above a clump of mid-green leaves. Reliably raised from seed. May to September. **H × S** 60cm × 30cm. AGM

'Prinses Juliana' A very free-flowering plant with lots of tall stems carrying semi-double, orange flowers above a clump of upright, mid-green leaves. May to August. **H × S** 50cm × 60cm

'Totally Tangerine' Tall, well-branched stems of soft-orange flowers, faintly tinged red, are carried on upright stems above a dense clump of mid-green leaves. Said to be the most free-flowering *Geum*, I find it no more floriferous than 'Prinses Juliana'. May to September. **H × S** 60cm × 60cm

GILLENIA (Bowman's root)

trifoliata An all-round excellent perennial that grows into a glorious, upright, bushy plant with frothy sprays of small, fluttering, white flowers borne on slender, branched, red stems. The oval, pointed, mid-green leaves turn a beautiful glowing orange in autumn. June to August. **H × S** 90cm × 75cm. AGM

Needs Well-drained soil in sun to partial shade
Great for Middle of a border
Bees & Butterflies Bees
For Cutting No
Care Trouble free and long-lived

Geum 'Mai Tai'

Geum 'Marmalade'

Geum 'Mrs J. Bradshaw'

Geum 'Prinses Juliana'

Geum 'Totally Tangerine'

Gillenia trifoliata

Hakonechloa macra 'Aureola'

Helenium 'Can Can'

Helenium 'Dunkle Pracht'

Helenium 'Riverton Beauty'

Helenium 'Sahin's Early Flowerer'

HAKONECHLOA

macra **'Aureola'** A lovely, fluffy, tufted grass with yellow-lined, soft-green leaves. Slender stems of tiny, soft-brown flowers are almost hidden among the foliage. In autumn the leaves turn red. August to September. **H × S** 45cm × 45cm. AGM

Needs Very well-drained soil that remains moist in sun or partial shade
Great for Containers or edging
Bees & Butterflies No
For Cutting No
Care Cut back in spring

HELENIUM (Sneezeweed)

Nothing can compare to a swathe of heleniums for late-summer colour. The daisy flowers have frilly petals that often change from one bright shade to another with age. The centres, too, begin as a flat disc then grow into a pouffe-like dome, ringed by yellow stamens. The flowers are held on rigid, branched stems above a slowly expanding clump of long, mid-green leaves that rarely needs extra support.

Needs Well-drained soil that remains moist in sun
Great for Back of the border
Bees & Butterflies Yes
For Cutting Yes
Care Be restrained when dividing clumps. Otherwise trouble free

'Can Can' These red-flushed, bright-yellow flowers seem to swirl like a dancer's skirt. July to September. **H × S** 75cm × 60cm

'Dunkle Pracht' A variety with frilly dark red petals that fade to orange. July to September. **H × S** 120cm × 75cm. AGM

'Moerheim Beauty' A deservedly popular plant with warm, reddish-brown flowers fading to burnt orange. July to September. **H × S** 90cm × 75cm. AGM

'Riverton Beauty' Petals of a pure, bright yellow surround dark-bronze domes. July to September. **H × S** 120cm × 75cm

'Rubinzwerg' A variety with brick-red flowers that turn orange over time. July to September. **H × S** 75cm × 60cm. AGM

'Sahin's Early Flowerer' This has yellow flowers flecked with red, that turn red. July to September. **H × S** 90cm × 75cm. AGM

'Waltraut' From a distance the yellow flowers, which deepen to soft red, appear bronze. July to September. **H × S** 90cm × 75cm. AGM

'Wyndley' The relaxed, yellow flowers are marked with the occasional fleck of red. July to September. **H × S** 90cm × 75cm

Helenium 'Rubinzwerg'

Helenium 'Waltraut'

Helenium 'Wyndley'

Helenium 'Moerheim Beauty'

Helianthus 'Lemon Queen'

Helleborus argutifolius

Helleborus foetidus

Helleborus niger

Helleborus × *hybridus*

HELIANTHUS (Perennial sunflower)

'Lemon Queen' This big, vigorous plant carries bright-lemon daisies on stiff, upright stems with dark green leaves. In time, it will form an imposing upright clump. August to September. **H × S** 180cm × 105cm. AGM

Needs Well-drained soil in sun
Great for Very back of the border
Bees & Butterflies Yes
For Cutting No
Care Trouble free and, despite being tall, it needs no staking

HELLEBORUS

Invaluable for late-winter and early-spring colour and form, hellebores add a touch of classic beauty to the barrenness of a winter garden. Elegant, simply shaped flowers emerge from clumps of handsome, evergreen leaves. Perfect for shadier spots and some adapt well to containers.

Needs Well-drained soil that remains moist in full or partial shade
Great for A shady or woodland garden
Bees & Butterflies No
For Cutting Yes
Care All varieties are slow to establish but are generally disease-free, although *H. niger* and × *hybridus* sometimes suffer from leaf spot. Removing the old leaves in early spring not only tidies up a plant, it helps to reduce the risk of blotches

argutifolius Clusters of large, cupped, soft-green flowers are carried on thick stems above a dome of evergreen, leathery, deep-green leaves, serrated along the edges. March to April. **H × S** 75cm × 60cm. AGM

foetidus (Stinking hellebore) Our native hellebore (rarely seen growing wild) has big sprays of small, ball-shaped, soft-green buds carried on thick, upright stems. These open into cupped flowers above finger-like, deep-green leaves, that smell like roast beef when bruised. February to April.
H × S 80cm × 60cm. AGM

× *hybridus* (Lenten rose) A variable, seed-raised plant. The large, open flowers in shades through maroon to white, many of them freckled inside, emerge just above divided, dark green leaves. There are also named varieties, including doubles and yellow forms, but these can be tricky to grow. February to March. **H × S** 60cm × 60cm

niger (Christmas rose) Once the most popular hellebore, the open, pure-white flowers are carried on short stems. The leaves, which form an open clump, are not reliably evergreen. February to March.
H × S 45cm × 45cm

HEMEROCALLIS (Daylily)

Reliable, easy to grow and difficult to kill, these tough plants are ideal for those who want a perennial they can forget about. The flowers of daylilies are produced in great abundance, each stem loaded with flower buds that open one a day over many weeks. The flowers are trumpet shaped or flat and range in size from 5cm to 15cm in diameter. They are carried on strong stems that emerge from a thick clump of long, slender, mid-green leaves. From over 3,000 listed by the Royal Horticultural Society, I have tried to select plants that are easily obtained and represent the enormous variety on offer.

Needs Any soil, except boggy, in sun, partial shade, or shade
Great for All areas of the garden and border
Bees & Butterflies No
For Cutting No
Care In some parts of the UK, the grubs of a tiny fly that is attracted to daylilies, the gall midge, can hatch inside the flower buds. These subsequently become deformed and fail to open. We had one instance at the nursery so I swiftly removed the buds and burnt them. The later flowers opened successfully without any deformities

'Always Afternoon' This large-flowered variety has broad, scented blooms in a rich pink with a striking maroon-purple ring around a green centre. They are held just above the leaves. July to August. **H × S** 75cm × 75cm. AGM

'Bonanza' An old, reliable variety with large, scented, rich-yellow, starry flowers marked inside with maroon. They are carried on tall stems high above the foliage. July to August. **H × S** 85cm × 60cm

'Cartwheels' A plant that really stands out from a distance. The big, flat, rich-yellow flowers sit just above the leaves. July to August. **H × S** 75cm × 75cm

'Catherine Woodbery' One of the first pink varieties I grew – at that time very popular for its large, open flowers. Three of the petals are lilac pink, three are pale pink. July to August. **H × S** 75cm × 75cm

'Cherry Eyed Pumpkin' A cheerful plant with big, rich-orange flowers, each displaying a pale-maroon halo around a yellow throat. The flower petals are ruffled at the edges. July to August. **H × S** 75cm × 60cm. AGM

'Crimson Pirate' The small, starry, trumpet-shaped, bright-red flowers have yellow centres. They are produced in succession on slender stems high above the leaves. July to August. **H × S** 75cm × 75cm

Hemerocallis 'Always Afternoon'

Hemerocallis 'Bonanza'

Hemerocallis 'Cartwheels'

Hemerocallis 'Catherine Woodbery'

Hemerocallis 'Cherry Eyed Pumpkin'

Hemerocallis 'Crimson Pirate'

Hemerocallis 'Custard Candy'

Hemerocallis 'Ed Murray'

Hemerocallis 'El Desperado'

Hemerocallis fulva 'Flore Pleno'

Hemerocallis 'Gentle Shepherd'

'Custard Candy' An extremely floriferous plant. The small, round, soft-yellow flowers have a maroon circle round the throat. They cover a neatly domed clump of leaves. July to August. **H × S** 60cm × 60cm. AGM

'Ed Murray' Good enough to eat, its velvety flowers are darkest red and not over-large. They are carried in clusters of two or three on slender stems high above the leaves. July to August. **H × S** 75cm × 75cm

'El Desperado' A charming plant that produces clusters of the large, soft-yellow flowers just above the leaves. Each flower has deep-maroon flares, a lime-green centre, and lightly laced edges to the petals. July to August. **H × S** 70cm × 70cm

fulva **'Flore Pleno'** This old variety has large, trumpet-shaped, deep-orange flowers that feature an inner set of petals, making this a double form. Each of the petals is brushed with red. June to August. **H × S** 105cm × 75cm

'Gentle Shepherd' One of the first large, near-white flowers that I grew, although in reality the colour is nearer cream than white. The crêpe petals surround a lime-green throat. July to August. **H × S** 75cm × 75cm

'Grape Velvet' A small-flowered plant with muted-purple, trumpet-shaped blooms with paler mid-ribs and lime-green centres. The velvety-textured flowers sit just above the leaves. July to August. **H × S** 75cm × 75cm

'Happy Returns' As its name suggests, this is a very free-flowering daylily with small, yellow flowers carried just above a neat clump of leaves. Works well in a container. June to August. **H × S** 45cm × 45cm

'James Marsh' A handsome plant with large, trumpet-shaped, true-red flowers carried just above a clump of deep-green leaves. July to August. **H × S** 70cm × 60cm

'Joan Senior' The creamy, open blooms fade to almost white with time. The flowers are held just above the leaves. July to August. **H × S** 65cm × 60cm

'Lacy Doily' Many double daylilies have rather untidy-looking flowers. This variety produces neat heads of small, pretty, pale-pink flowers, overlaid with cream. July to August. **H × S** 60cm × 60cm

'Lavender Showstopper' An aptly named plant that I really admire. The large, open, pale-pink flowers with lime-yellow centres are delicately edged by a wash of purple. The flowers are carried on widely branched stems. Well worth seeking out. July to August. **H × S** 90cm × 75cm

Hemerocallis 'Grape Velvet'

Hemerocallis 'Happy Returns'

Hemerocallis 'James Marsh'

Hemerocallis 'Joan Senior'

Hemerocallis 'Lacy Doily'

Hemerocallis 'Lavender Showstopper'

Hemerocallis 'Lemon Bells'

Hemerocallis 'Lilting Lavender'

Hemerocallis 'Ming Porcelain'

Hemerocallis 'Night Beacon'

Hemerocallis 'Pandora's Box'

Hemerocallis 'Pardon Me'

'Lemon Bells' For the best scent, choose the yellow varieties of daylily. This one produces lots of heavily lemon-scented, small, bright-yellow, trumpet-shaped flowers on slender stems. June to August. **H × S** 75cm × 75cm

'Lilting Lavender' Daylily fanciers refer to the form of this flower as spider-shaped. The big, lavender-pink blooms display long petals and soft-lemon centres. They are carried on really tall stems above the leaves. July to August. **H × S** 90cm × 75cm

'Ming Porcelain' The wide, soft-apricot flowers have a yellow throat. They are carried on short stems just above the leaves. July to August. **H × S** 60cm × 60cm

'Night Beacon' A variety with open, trumpet-shaped, rich pink-purple flowers. Each petal has a distinct white mid-rib and a big, green-yellow centre. The flowers are carried on slender stems. July to August. **H × S** 70cm × 60cm

'Pandora's Box' A free-flowering, low-growing plant. Clusters of small, soft-cream flowers with maroon centres open on upright stems just above the leaves. July to August. **H × S** 45cm × 60cm

'Pardon Me' One of the best of the small-flowered, rich reds. Blooms are produced one at a time over weeks on upright, slender stems above a short clump of leaves. July to September. **H × S** 45cm × 45cm

'Pink Damask' This classic variety bears smooth, trumpet-shaped, rich salmon-pink flowers. These are produced in great abundance even in a shady spot. July to August. **H × S** 80cm × 75cm. AGM

'Spider Man' A lovely variety. Very big, star-shaped, rich deep-red flowers with little, yellow centres add impact to a border, especially when combined with other hot-coloured plants. July to August. **H × S** 90cm × 75cm. AGM

'Strawberry Candy' One of the free-flowering 'Candy' series. Its neat, rounded, apricot flowers with frilled edges are marked with a red inner ring. They are carried just above a broad clump of leaves. July to August. **H × S** 60cm × 60cm. AGM

'Summer Wine' A compact plant with lots of mid-sized, neat, trumpet-shaped flowers borne above the leaves. The soft pink-purple hue literally glows. July to August. **H × S** 60cm × 60cm

HESPERANTHA

coccinea **'Major'** Once listed as *Schizostylis*, this needs a warm spot where its large, silky, crimson flowers inject a welcome burst of colour. They sit at the top of graceful stems, above a clump of grassy, mid-green leaves that are just about evergreen. October to November. **H × S** 75cm × 45cm. AGM

Needs Soil that retains moisture in sun
Great for Front of border
Bees & Butterflies Yes
For Cutting Yes
Care Given a sunny, sheltered position in soil that does not dry out, the clump will slowly get bigger and better

Hemerocallis 'Spider Man'

Hemerocallis 'Pink Damask'

Hemerocallis 'Strawberry Candy'

Hemerocallis 'Summer Wine'

Hesperantha coccinea 'Major'

Heuchera 'Obsidian'

Heuchera 'Plum Pudding'

Heuchera 'Strawberry Swirl'

Heuchera villosa 'Palace Purple'

Hosta 'Frances Williams'

Hosta 'Halcyon' (Tardiana Group)

HEUCHERA (Coralbells)

There are hundreds of heucheras, some with evergreen foliage in greens, reds, and even orange. Some are so similar it is difficult to tell them apart, others are not very hardy, and some are hard to combine with other perennials. All produce spikes of tiny, funnel-shaped flowers on very slender stems above a dense mound of vine-shaped leaves.

Needs Well-drained soil in sun or partial shade
Great for Front of the border and pots
Bees & Butterflies No
For Cutting Yes
Care May be attacked by vine weevil. Some varieties dislike wet soils

'Obsidian' A really dark plant sending out smooth, almost black leaves that form a neat dome. Wispy spikes of tiny, cream flowers are carried on slender stems. July to September. **H × S** 60cm × 30cm

'Plum Pudding' The large, glossy, deep plum-coloured leaves are tinted with grey, and create a handsome mound. The tiny, white flowers on dark stems are not particularly impressive. July to September. **H × S** 60cm × 30cm

'Strawberry Swirl' Flowery in comparison with other varieties, sending up frothy stems of delicate-pink blooms. These sit above a loose mound of jagged, rich-green leaves. June to August. **H × S** 60cm × 30cm

villosa **'Palace Purple'** From loose mounds of large, mahogany-red leaves with bronze tints, airy spikes of white flowers emerge. July to August. **H × S** 60cm × 45cm

HOSTA

The main reason to grow these striking plants is for the big handsome leaves, although the flowers are also ornamental and are often scented. They are a must if you garden in shady, damp spots. Sadly, they seem to be one of the go-to plants for slugs, but there are steps you can take.

Needs Best in soil that remains moist, but will grow in any soil, except very dry
Great for Shady borders and containers
Bees & Butterflies bees
For Cutting Yes
Care If your garden is regularly visited by slugs and snails, grow hostas in pots and stand them on slabs or gravel. Also choose varieties with thicker leaves, which tend to be more resistant to slugs

'Frances Williams' This very large variety has broad, yellow-edged, blue-green leaves that send up stout stems of white flowers. July to August. **H × S** 90cm × 80cm. AGM

Hosta 'Krossa Regal'

Hosta 'Patriot'

Hosta sieboldiana var. *elegans*

Hosta 'Sum and Substance'

Inula hookeri

Inula magnifica

'Halcyon' (Tardiana Group) Rising from a compact mound of heart-shaped, blue-grey leaves, the short stems are packed with big, trumpet-shaped, lilac flowers. July to August. **H × S** 45cm × 60cm. AGM

'Krossa Regal' This elegantly shaped plant has deeply veined, grey-green leaves that arch upwards then splay out. Lilac, bell-shaped flowers are carried on long stems. July to August. **H × S** 120cm × 60cm. AGM

'Patriot' This forms a low clump of eye-catching, oval, grass-green leaves, broadly edged with white. The bell-like flowers are a light lavender shade. July to August. **H × S** 75cm × 75cm. AGM

sieboldiana* var. *elegans A sizeable plant when mature with round, deeply veined and puckered, blue-green leaves. The thick spikes of lilac flowers are outward facing. July to August. **H × S** 90cm × 80cm. AGM

'Sum and Substance' Magnificent in a pot, this produces very large, deeply ridged, yellow leaves and lilac flowers. July to August. **H × S** 105cm × 90cm. AGM

INULA (Fleabane)

A small group of bright yellow, daisy-flowered plants with fine rays surrounding the centre. The leaves are big and hairy.

Needs Well-drained soil that does not dry out, including clay soils
Great for Front and back of the border
Bees & Butterflies Yes
For Cutting Yes
Care Trouble free but can spread rapidly

hookeri Ideal for cool moist soils. The flowers are carried proudly above a broad, mounding clump of leaves. July to August. **H × S** 75cm × 70cm

magnifica A majestic plant with large, golden flowers on tall, leafy stems that often need no staking to stay upright. July to August. **H × S** 200cm × 90cm

Iris

Irises have the most colourful and flamboyant flowers of all the perennials. Ranging from white to almost black, every possible tone is available except red – a colour that does not exist in the iris family. The flowers are three dimensional in structure with large, thick petals that are smooth or outrageously ruffled, and when planted in the garden, they always inject that 'wow' factor. Given the right conditions, they are easy to grow and there is a variety for every possible garden site and situation. And that's not all: with just a few plants, you can have irises in flower every month of the year.

The iris world is a large one with more than 200 species found throughout the Northern Hemisphere. The plants are classified according to how they grow below ground (rhizomes or bulbs), then, for gardening purposes, into two further groups – bearded or beardless. Beardless irises are the most numerous in terms of species, with varieties for every situation in the garden, but there is a much greater choice of flower colour and height when it comes to Bearded irises.

THE FLOWERS

The flowers of all irises are proportionally large when compared to the rest of the plant. They have six petals: three upper ones known as standards, and three lower petals called the falls. Bearded irises have what looks like a hairy caterpillar crawling out of the throat of the falls, and they take their name from this distinctive feature. The beards are replaced by a yellow flash, called a signal, on the flowers of beardless irises. These colourful devices – beards and signals – attract pollinating insects.

THE LEAVES

All irises produce long, pointed leaves. Those of bearded irises are sword-like and matt grey-green in colour. The leaves of beardless types are often shiny and mid- or soft green. In some, such as Pacific Coast irises, the leaves arch over, while Siberian iris leaves are ramrod straight and almost grass-like. All produce handsome clumps and are useful – I would even say essential – for complementing perennials with bigger, broader leaves.

THE ROOTS

Irises are tough, tolerant plants because they grow from either bulbs or rhizomes. These storage systems help the plant to survive in extreme conditions, including very dry and waterlogged soil.

The irises in this book all grow from rhizomes (*see* right). Found at the base of the leaves and flower stems, they are generally long and ridged. The rhizomes, from which the roots grow, are an underground extension of the flower stems.

Bearded irises growing in our field, June

The beard on a bearded iris

The signal on a beardless iris

The rhizome of a bearded iris

IRIS TERMS USED

FALLS The three lower petals

STANDARDS Three upper petals

BEARDS A 'caterpillar' of hairs on the falls of bearded irises

SIGNAL The blaze of yellow on the falls of beardless irises

REMONTANT Flowering twice; first in late spring or early summer, and again from late summer onwards

DYKES A medal awarded to the best iris in Britain and in North America

IRISES FOR ALL SEASONS

By planting a combination of beardless and bearded irises, your garden can have irises in flower every month of the year. Although June is the month when most irises bloom, those types that flower in other months are listed below:

January
Iris unguicularis
February
Iris unguicularis
March
Standard dwarf bearded irises
April
Standard dwarf bearded irises
May
Standard dwarf bearded irises
Intermediate bearded irises
June
Intermediate bearded irises
Border bearded irises
Miniature tall bearded and tall bearded irises
Sibirica irises, *Iris pseudacorus*, *Iris ensata*
July
Spuria irises
August
Remontant bearded irises: standard dwarf and tall bearded irises
September
Remontant bearded irises: standard dwarf and tall bearded irises
October
Remontant bearded irises: tall bearded irises
November
Remontant bearded irises: tall bearded irises
December
Iris unguicularis

WHERE TO FIND IRIS TYPES

Bearded irises:		Beardless irises:	
Tall bearded irises	pp. 102–112	Sibirica	pp. 118–119
Median bearded irises	pp. 113–117	for damp soils	p. 120
		Pacific Coast and Spuria	p. 121

Many people know these big, flowered irises as 'flag' irises, the common name of the wild, yellow bog iris, *Iris pseudacorus*. Once only seen in shades of blue, purple, or white with a few yellows thrown in, today bearded iris flowers are found in almost every colour and combination except true red and black. The heights and flowering seasons vary so a garden can be blessed with bearded irises from March (in the most southerly counties) to November. In a perennial planting, the elegant, sword-like, grey-green leaves contrast well with leaves of other shapes.

GROWING BEARDED IRISES

Bearded irises like a well-drained, neutral soil. In really wet or very acid soils the rhizome can rot so severely that the plant will simply die. Bearded irises also need a lot of sun to 'bake' the rhizome, allowing it to heat up sufficiently to form flowers for the following year. However, I have also seen them flower in part-shade under tall trees in a south-facing border in southern England – albeit they were planted where slanting rays of sun could reach them. The plants may struggle in this location in cooler, more northerly counties.

Planting time

Traditionally, bearded irises are planted six weeks after flowering time, from July onwards. We don't start moving irises on the nursery until late August, after the hottest and driest days of the summer have passed. By then the rhizomes are fully matured and the ground, although it might be damper, is still warm. It is not wise to plant between late October and March because the dormant rhizome will sit in cold, wet soil and may rot. Irises can be planted in spring, but they are unlikely to flower the same summer.

Dividing

Irises that grow from rhizomes multiply by simply sending out new rhizomes. These spread outwards as they go, creating a fan shape, while leaving a gap in the middle. Eventually there are so many old rhizomes the plant will stop flowering. To keep plants vigorous, divide them every three years – or more often for very robust, smaller varieties.

To divide an old clump, dig it up and shake off the soil. Snap off any rhizome with a green top. Discard the other rhizomes; they won't flower again. Trim the roots of each remaining rhizome to make it easier to plant, and cut the leaves down to approximately the length of your hand. This will prevent the rhizome being loosened in windy weather. It doesn't matter whether the top of the leaves is cut straight or at an angle.

Grouping

Bearded irises can be grown as single specimens, but because each plant can take two or three years to create an impact, I prefer to plant them in groups of two or more – especially when grown among other perennials. To keep the rhizome from being swamped by surrounding plants, which will stop the iris from flowering, I like to create a 'wall' with the leaves. Simply plant the rhizomes in a triangle or circle with the tips facing each other. As bearded irises spread quite a bit, taller varieties should be placed about 30cm apart, while smaller ones can be as close as 23cm.

Planting

The all-important rhizome, which produces the flower, should always be planted shallowly. Dig a hole deep enough to take the roots and half of the rhizome. Put the roots and the bottom half of the rhizome into the hole and back fill, leaving just the top of the rhizome showing. Make sure you tuck all the roots into the ground: birds see stray ones as worms, tug at them, and lever the plant out of the soil.

Maintaining

In most cases, bearded irises do not need fertilising. If you want to, use a fertiliser that is very low in nitrogen and don't overdo it. Too much feeding, especially with a high-nitrogen fertiliser, will result in soft growth and probably cause the rhizome to rot.

In autumn you can remove any dead leaves. It is unnecessary to cut the leaves back earlier in the season, although it won't harm the plant.

Pests and Diseases

Bearded irises are generally robust although they may be attacked by slugs and snails (*see* p. 33). In prolonged wet periods, they can suffer from leaf spot (*see* p. 33). If the rhizome becomes soft and smelly, this is probably bacterial soft rot. It is easily sorted by simply cut out the affected part.

The fabulous purple-tinged buds of the tall bearded *Iris* 'Guatemala'

Iris rhizomes after two years

Late snow, even in April, won't harm irises

FLOWERS

Tall bearded irises can carry their big, showy flowers up the entire length of the thick flower stem, creating a colourful flower spike. Each bloom squeezes itself out of a 'socket' at the end of short branching side stems. Flowers appear in succession, each lasting for two to three days. Many modern varieties have three or four flowers per socket, so up to 16 flowers can be borne by a single plant in one flowering period. After three years, a plant may produce up to ten flowering stems.

Fragrance

Bearded irises can be really fragrant, many emitting a thick, sweet scent, rather like honey. But there are also lemon-, chocolate-, and spice-scented blooms. As with many plants, the fragrance is best and at its strongest on warm days.

If a flower is fragrant, it is indicated within the description, but here are a few varieties with specific scents:

- **Chocolate** *Iris* 'Dusky Challenger'
- **Daffodil** *Iris* 'Spring Madness'
- **Lemon** *Iris* 'Godfrey Owen'
- **Orange** *Iris* 'Cordoba'
- **Spicy** *Iris* 'Annabel Jane'

Breeder

Most cultivated irises have been raised by a specialist or enthusiast. In the following descriptions, the name of the breeder has been included after the plant name, along with the year it was registered with the American Iris Society. For example, *Iris* 'Annabel Jane' (Dodsworth 1973).

Iris 'Dude Ranch' can have between eight and ten flowers per stem

FLOWERING TIMES

When a bearded iris flowers depends on where you garden. At our nursery, in the middle of the country, they usually start to bloom around early May. However, if you are further south or north, flowering can be ten days earlier or later. In warm springs, I have seen the shortest varieties start blooming in late March; after cold springs, the tallest may not finish flowering until early July.

In the 1950s, to help both gardeners and breeders, the American Iris Society grouped the many bearded iris varieties according to height and time of flowering as follows:

Tall Bearded (TB)
Producing the largest flowers, these irises are the last to bloom. They can be grown in their own bed, as a focal point, or mixed with other plants.
Flowering Late May to late June
Height Over 71cm

The four groups below are collectively known as Median Bearded Irises (see pp. 113–117).

Border Bearded (BB)
Coming into flower around the same time as TB irises, these are really shorter versions of TB irises. They grow more like IB irises, however, and are vigorous enough to grow in a mixed border.
Flowering Early to mid-June
Height 38cm to 71cm

Miniature Tall Bearded (MTB)
These flower around the same time as BB and TB irises. The blooms are small and delicate, as are the flower stems, but they work well near the front of the border.
Flowering Early to mid-June
Height 38cm to 71cm

Intermediate Bearded (IB)
Blooming just after SDB irises, the flowers of this group are larger and carried above the leaves. Being vigorous, they happily grow with other perennials.
Flowering Late May to mid-June
Height 38cm to 71cm

Standard Dwarf Bearded (SDB)
These have small flowers that sit just above a broad clump of leaves and are ideal for the front of a border.
Flowering Mid-April to early May
Height 20cm to 38cm

DYKES MEDAL

Since 1927, this medal has been awarded annually in the USA, occasionally in the UK, to the best iris following trials lasting some years. Winners of the medal, with the year, have been included, because more often than not they are excellent plants.

Tall bearded iris (TB) *Iris* 'Valerie Joyce'

Standard dwarf bearded iris (SDB)
Iris 'Sapphire Gem'

Iris 'Jesse's Song' (TB) Dykes Medal winner 1990

Iris 'Afternoon in Rio'

TALL BEARDED IRISES

The most flamboyant of all bearded irises, these carry their blooms on thick, upright stems high above the clump of leaves. Flowering time is from late May to mid June, with particular varieties blooming early, mid-season, or late within this period.

'Afternoon in Rio' (Schreiner 2005) The frilly, broad flowers are an unusual violet-purple with brown-rimmed falls and a small white patch in front of each bronze beard. Mid to late. **H** 90cm

'Aggressively Forward' (Innerst 1995) A heavily scented variety. The standards are corn-yellow and the falls a softer yellow edged with maroon, with spots of colour on the falls. The beards are gold. Mid. **H** 90cm

'Annabel Jane' (Dodsworth 1973) Raised in windy Britain, this lovely plant has robust stems. The lilac flowers are heavily ruffled and spicy scented. Dykes 1977. Mid. **H** 91cm

'Before the Storm' (Innerst 1988) Formerly one of the darkest irises with entirely purple-black flowers that are smooth and wavy. Dykes 1996. Mid to late. **H** 90cm

'Best Bet' (Schreiner 1988) A nice plant with ruffled pale-blue standards, flushed at the base with purple, royal-blue falls, and short, blue beards. Early. Remontant. **H** 90cm

'Bethany Claire' (Zurbrigg 1984) The scented, deep-violet flowers are large and uniformly coloured. They have short, white beards. Early. Remontant. **H** 102cm

'Blackberry Tease' (Johnson 2003) This nicely shaped, scented, blue-purple flower has falls that are almost white with a light wash of yellow. Early to mid. **H** 97cm

Iris 'Aggressively Forward'

Iris 'Before the Storm'

Iris 'Annabel Jane'

Iris 'Best Bet'

Iris 'Bethany Claire'

Iris 'Blackberry Tease'

'Blue Note Blues' (Ernst 1997) A free-flowering plant with scented, ruffled, mid-blue flowers. These are paler around the edges and the white beards are tipped with orange. Mid. **H** 94cm

'Blue Rhythm' (Whiting 1945) This classic variety has lots of smoothly shaped, lemon-scented, cornflower-blue flowers. The falls are a little darker in colour than the standards. Dykes 1950. Mid. **H** 110cm

'Braithwaite' (Randall 1952) A tried-and-tested plant with long, velvety-purple falls, paler around the edges, and lilac-white, upright standards that touch at the top. The beards are short and yellow. Late. **H** 84cm

'Breakers' (Schreiner 1987) The tightly ruffled, true-blue flowers have bright-blue beards with yellow tips. Mid. **H** 94cm

'Caliente' (Luihn 1967) There are no red-bearded irises, but this one comes quite close. The gently ruffled, scented, rich red-brown flowers have flaring, rounded falls with short, burnt-orange beards. Mid to late. **H** 97cm

'Carnaby' (Schreiner 1973) A distinctly feminine plant with frilly, lightly scented flowers. The peach-pink standards are flushed with lilac and the rose-purple falls are banded with soft peach. It has soft orange beards. Late. **H** 89cm

'Celebration Song' (Schreiner 1993) Ruffled, scented flowers with pale lilac falls contrast with soft peach-pink standards and orange beards. The flowers tend to be a darker shade when they first open. Dykes 2003. Early to late. **H** 94cm

Iris 'Blue Note Blues'

Iris 'Blue Rhythm'

Iris 'Braithwaite'

Iris 'Breakers'

Iris 'Caliente'

Iris 'Carnaby'

Iris 'Celebration Song'

Iris 'Change of Pace'

Iris 'Chasing Rainbows'

'Change of Pace' (Schreiner 1991) Early blooming with large, scented flowers. The rosy standards sparkle and the white falls are broadly edged and peppered with deep rosy-mauve. A great combination. Early to mid. **H** 89cm

'Chasing Rainbows' (Hager 1995) Ruffled and strongly scented. The soft-violet falls have paler centres and a wash of buff-peach along the edges. The standards are also buff-peach, stained with lilac from the base, and the beards are orange. Mid. **H** 81cm

'Cheap Frills' (Black 2009) Perfectly shaped, the scented, soft tangerine-orange flowers have buff speckles on the falls, fading to white in front of the tangerine beards. Early to late. **H** 97cm

'Circle of Light' (Black 2009) Large, beautifully formed flowers with shiny, deepest purple-blue petals sit squarely on tall, sturdy stems. Mid to late. **H** 99cm

'City Lights' (Dunn 1990) A variety with scented, purest-violet flowers and broad, white beards that merge with the pale throat of the falls. The standards are flushed at the base with white. Mid. **H** 94cm

'Coal Seams' (Schreiner 2013) As its name suggests, this is one of the 'blackest' irises. Perfectly shaped and ruffled flowers have shiny, dark-purple standards, velvety black falls, and dark purple beards. Mid. **H** 104cm

'Coalignition' (Burseen 1991) A luxurious, spicy-scented flower with velvety, black-grape falls, silky wine-red standards, and eye-catching, mustard-coloured beards. Early to mid. Remontant. **H** 91cm

Iris 'Cheap Frills'

Iris 'Circle of Light'

Iris 'City Lights'

Iris 'Coal Seams'

Iris 'Coalignition'

Iris 'Copatonic'

Iris 'Crowned Heads'

'Copatonic' (Blyth 1995) Sweetly yet also sharply scented, the large, ruffled flowers have velvety, russet-brown falls edged with a band of deep caramel – the same colour as the standards. Early to mid. **H** 86cm

'Cordoba' (Ghio 1998) Not acknowledged as a remontant iris, but we find it reliably so. The delightful orange flowers are also orange-scented with short, bright-orange beards. Early to late. Remontant. **H** 91cm

'Crowned Heads' (Keppel 1997) Irises bred with darker standards than falls are fairly new. This excellent, scented variety has violet-blue standards and pale-blue falls; both are veined with blue. The beards are a soft blue. Dykes 2004. Mid. **H** 97cm

'Decadence' (Blyth 2001) Loved by iris breeders for its flamboyant flowers with frilly, apricot standards, dark magenta falls, and orange beards. The parent of many wonderful varieties. Mid. **H** 96cm

'Discovered Treasure' (Johnson 2005) Free-flowering and sweetly scented, the soft-pink standards are gently flushed with violet. The violet falls display bright-orange beards. Mid. **H** 97cm

'Drama Queen' (Keppel 2004) This amazing flower has uniformly deep-burgundy standards. The falls are patterned with veins of sand-yellow and the beards are burnt-orange. Dykes 2011. Mid. **H** 97cm

'Dusky Challenger' (Schreiner 1986) One of the most popular irises in the US with very large, nicely ruffled, shiny, dark navy-blue flowers. The scent is heavy, sharp, and reminiscent of hot chocolate. Dykes 1992. Mid to late. **H** 99cm

Iris 'Cordoba'

Iris 'Decadence'

Iris 'Discovered Treasure'

Iris 'Drama Queen'

Iris 'Dusky Challenger'

'English Cottage' (Zurbrigg 1976) This most reliably remontant iris is also almost the first to bloom. White, heavily scented flowers are lightly speckled with soft violet and the white beards are tipped with yellow towards the back. Early. Remontant. **H** 98cm

'Flavescens' (De Candolle 1813) This old variety produces abundant small, scented, soft-yellow flowers that open all the way down the stem over a long period. Early to mid. **H** 89cm

'Florentina' Historically, this was the most important iris to be grown commercially. For centuries, orris root was made from the rhizomes in Italy. The sweet-scented powder is still sometimes added to pot pourri. The white blooms are lightly tinged with blue and have white beards. Early. **H** 75cm. AGM

'Florentine Silk' (Keppel 2004) Frilly, soft-peach, violet-tinged standards and violet falls that pale to peach around the edges make a striking combination. The beards are violet at the front, orange at the back. Dykes 2012. Mid to late. **H** 102cm

'Fogbound' (Keppel 1997) A ruffled, scented flower with pale-purple standards stained darker at the base. The falls are paler lilac and have short, white beards touched with orange at the back. Mid. **H** 107cm

'Foreign Legion' (Keppel 2002) Sweetly scented with ruffled, yellow-apricot standards, maroon falls and fat, vibrant-orange beards. Mid to late. **H** 99cm

'Fortunate Son' (Schreiner 2006) A richly coloured plant with velvety, orange-scented, pure-burgundy flowers and short, purple beards. Early to mid. **H** 94cm

Iris 'English Cottage'

Iris flavescens

Iris 'Florentina'

Iris 'Florentine Silk'

Iris 'Fogbound'

Iris 'Foreign Legion'

Iris 'Fortunate Son'

'Godfrey Owen' (Owen 1986) Raised by Margaret Owen, a wonderful (sometimes formidable) plantswoman from Shropshire who encouraged many, including myself. Margaret was deeply disappointed when her lovely, lemon-scented iris won only third prize in Italy's most prestigious iris show. Lightly ruffled, it has pale-yellow standards and yellow-edged, white falls with bright yellow beards. Early to late. **H** 91cm

'Going My Way' (Gibson 1971) A popular variety since the 1970s, its purple standards are lightly spotted with white from the base, and the white falls are broadly edged with dark purple. The thick petals are lightly scented and gently ruffled. Mid. **H** 94cm

'Golden Encore' (Jones 1972) To an iris fancier, these bright-yellow flowers are 'tailored'. Smoothly shaped, there is just a hint of white on the falls, in front of the yellow beards. Early. Remontant. **H** 89cm

'Good Looking' (Schreiner 1995) The colour of the slightly scented, ruffled flowers is a rather dusky grey-violet with flashes of violet extending down from short, violet beards. Early to mid. **H** 94cm

'Habit' (P. Black 1999) Sometimes a little fussy about where it grows, this big, fragrant flower has velvety, purple-black falls, soft-lilac standards, flecked with violet, and gold beards. Mid. **H** 86cm

'Happenstance' (Keppel 2000) Although not known for its toughness, this is still probably the hardiest and most vigorous pink variety around. The distinctively scented, lightly ruffled, soft-pink flowers have laced petal edges and fat, coral-coloured beards. Mid. **H** 95cm

Iris 'Godfrey Owen'

Iris 'Going My Way'

Iris 'Golden Encore'

Iris 'Good Looking'

Iris 'Habit'

Iris 'Happenstance'

Iris 'Ink Patterns'

'Ink Patterns' (Johnson 2007) This exquisite white iris displays blue-purple stippling and fine etching around the petal edges. The beards are soft blue. Mid. **H** 91cm

'Jane Phillips' (Graves 1946) Justly celebrated, this pale-blue, scented variety has petals like crêpe paper and white beards. The grey-green leaves are disease resistant. Over the years it has been the parent of many good irises. Mid. **H** 91cm

'Joyful Skies' (Schreiner 2004) Bearded irises in shades of blue blend easily with other flowering perennials. This lovely plant has soft-blue flowers with wavy petals. The falls fade to white around the white beards. Early to mid. **H** 91cm

'Jurassic Park' (Lauer 1995) A distinctive, scented bi-colour, this has light mustard-yellow standards. The violet falls are paler around the edges and the sparse beards are yellow. Early to mid. **H** 91cm

'Lovely Again' (Smith 1963) Guaranteed to re-bloom, this iris has delicate-textured, smoothly shaped, scented, lavender flowers that soften in colour as the plant ages. The beards are yellow. Early. Remontant. **H** 76cm

'Lovely Senorita' (Schreiner 2002) Lightly ruffled and attractive, the large flowers have deep-orange standards and burnt-orange falls. These are flushed with violet in front of the short, bushy, tangerine beards. Mid to late. **H** 104cm

'Miami Beach' (Keppel 2004) A gorgeous fragrant, smooth, yellow-flowered variety with gently ruffled petals. There is a small white patch in front of the bushy, orange beards. Mid. **H** 102cm

Iris 'Jane Phillips'

Iris 'Jurassic Park'

Iris 'Joyful Skies'

Iris 'Lovely Again'

Iris 'Lovely Senorita'

Iris 'Miami Beach'

'Millennium Sunrise' (Schreiner 2000) Still one of the best orange varieties we grow, it has large, ruffled petals and rich-orange beards. Early to late. **H** 99cm

'New Face' (Black 2008) An exquisite combination of colours. The ruffled, scented flowers have lilac standards, dark rose-pink falls, and lilac beards. Early to late. **H** 91cm

'Out of the Dark' (Black 2007) This handsome, heavily scented iris has thick, ruffled petals. The standards are rosy-purple and the soft-yellow falls are heavily banded and stippled with purple. It has bright orange beards. Mid to late. **H** 102cm

pallida Widespread in gardens throughout Western Europe, this has scented, pale violet-blue flowers with white beards. The flowers withstand bad weather and the handsome grey-green leaves are disease resistant. Early. **H** 110cm

'Parisian Dawn' (Keppel 2005) Glamorous and flouncy, the soft-peach flowers are broadly washed with a delicate grey-lilac along the edges of the falls. The thick beards are orange. Mid to late. **H** 91cm

'Party's Over' (Meek 2005) An eye-catching plant with tightly ruffled flowers. These have soft violet-blue standards, white falls heavily washed with corn-yellow from the edges, and white beards. Early to mid. **H** 86cm

'Pipes of Pan' (Brown 1963) An old, but floriferous plant. Its smoothly shaped flowers have mauve falls that are paler along the edges. The standards are buff and flushed with mauve towards the base. Mid to late. **H** 99cm

Iris 'Millennium Sunrise'

Iris 'New Face'

Iris 'Out of the Dark'

Iris pallida

Iris 'Parisian Dawn'

Iris 'Party's Over'

Iris 'Pipes of Pan'

Iris 'Red Revival'

Iris 'Ringo'

Iris 'Rio Rojo'

Iris 'Sam Carne'

Iris 'Share the Spirit'

Iris 'Shurton Inn'

Iris 'Silverado'

'Red Revival' (Preston 1975) Despite its name, this has bronze standards, brown falls heavily veined with yellow, and deep-orange beards. The colour is much richer in autumn. Early. Remontant. **H** 76cm

'Ringo' (Shoop 1979) Although not the most free-flowering iris, this has attractive, gently ruffled flowers with clean, white standards, rose-purple falls rimmed with white, and tangerine beards. Mid. **H** 76cm

'Rio Rojo' (Schreiner 2009) A simply gorgeous iris with smooth, rich claret-red flowers, gently ruffled along the edges and blue-purple beards. Early to mid. **H** 97cm

'Sam Carne' (Nichol 1985) This vigorous plant was raised in Wales and multiplies readily. The colour of the ruffled, violet-blue flowers sits at the mid-point between soft- and dark blue. Mid. **H** 97cm

'Share the Spirit' (Grosvenor 1998) A lovely variety that cropped up by mistake on one of our Chelsea Flower Show stands. The thick, ruffled, soft-blue petals are washed with purple, have short, blue beards, and are carried on sturdy stems. Late. **H** 89cm

'Shurton Inn' (Bartlett 1994) This English variety was named after a pub the breeder visited. It has flaring, soft-brown falls, white standards flushed with ochre, and dark yellow beards. Mid to late. **H** 86cm

'Silverado' (Schreiner 1987) Beautifully shaped, large, and slightly scented, the soft-blue flowers display delicate touches of purple. Dykes 1994. Mid. **H** 97cm

Iris 'Snowy Owl'

Iris 'Stairway to Heaven'

'Snowy Owl' (Blodgett 1977) The toughest white variety I have grown. Its ruffled flowers are pure white and the white beards are very gently brushed with yellow. Mid. **H** 97cm

'Spring Madness' (Johnson 2009) Delicious is the only word for this daffodil-scented flower with thick petals that withstand bad weather. It has white standards and white-rimmed, yellow falls finely etched with lines of brown-purple. Late. **H** 89cm

'Stairway to Heaven' (Lauer 1992) A variety with lots of large flowers carried right to the bottom of the strong stems. Creamy-white standards rise above lavender-blue falls and yellow-tipped, white beards. Dykes 2000. Early to mid. **H** 102cm

'Star Shine' (Wills 1949) The flowers of this old, strong growing variety have soft yellow standards that pale towards the edges. Lilac-flushed, white falls display dark yellow wings either side of the yellow beards. Mid to late. **H** 102cm

'Stellar Lights' (Aitken 1985) Re-flowering reliably, this plant has ruffled, shiny, dark violet flowers. The falls have central, white patches in front of the white beards. Mid to late. Remontant. **H** 97cm

'Sunblaze' (Keppel 2003) Although many yellow irises are not hardy, this one is. It has scented, vibrant-yellow flowers with thick petals. The flowers are carried on strong stems. Early to mid. **H** 98cm

'Superstition' (Schreiner 1977) Reliable and free-flowering, this variety has lightly ruffled, purple-black flowers with a lovely silky sheen. Mid. **H** 91cm

Iris 'Spring Madness'

Iris 'Star Shine'

Iris 'Stellar Lights'

Iris 'Sunblaze'

Iris 'Superstition'

Iris 'Supreme Sultan'

Iris 'Sweet Musette'

Iris 'Swingtown'

'Supreme Sultan' (Schreiner 1987) Even though this variety has large flowers, the stems don't usually topple over. Flaring, red-brown falls display beards of deep gold and the ruffled standards are golden yellow. Mid to late. **H** 102cm

'Sweet Musette' (Schreiner 1986) As laced and frilled as a Victorian lady's underwear, this feminine flower has soft-peach standards, serrated along the edges. The pink-lavender falls are flushed with lavender and the beards are coral-red. Mid to late. **H** 94cm

'Swingtown' (Schreiner 1996) Almost the last tall bearded iris to bloom, this has heavily scented, very ruffled flowers on well-branched stems. The colour is vibrant blue-purple and the dark purple beards are V-shaped. Late. **H** 91cm

'Tall Chief' (DeForest 1955) Despite being over 50 years old, this is a really free-flowering plant with very lightly ruffled, mahogany-brown flowers and ginger beards. Mid to late. **H** 91cm

'Undercurrent' (Keppel 2004) This heavily scented, flouncy flower has soft-peach standards and rounded, soft-purple falls. These fade to delicate peach around the bushy, bright-orange beards. Mid to late. **H** 107cm

'Venita Faye' (Keppel 2007) A really pretty iris that is also heavily scented. The ruffled flowers have pale-pink standards, soft-lilac falls that pale in the centre, and white beards touched with coral at the back. Mid to late. **H** 97cm

Iris 'Venita Faye'

Iris 'Tall Chief'

Iris 'Undercurrent'

MEDIAN BEARDED IRISES

This group contains those bearded irises that are shorter than tall bearded irises. They all flower freely, but at different times. The varieties listed are among the most useful for all areas of the garden. I wouldn't recommend growing bearded irises in pots, but standard dwarf bearded types will survive happily in containers for a few years.

The different types of median bearded iris (with abbreviations used for each type) and their flowering periods are as follows:

Border Bearded (BB)
Flowering Early to mid-June

Miniature Tall Bearded (MTB)
Flowering Early to mid-June

Intermediate Bearded (IB)
Flowering Late May to mid-June

Standard Dwarf Bearded (SDB)
Flowering Mid-April to early May

For each plant listed, an indication is given as to whether it tends to bloom 'early', 'mid' or 'late' within its given flowering period. This should help you plan and choose varieties. Precise flowering times will, however, depend on your regional climate.

'Apricot Drops' (Aitken 1995) A prolific award-winning variety. The small, perfectly shaped, soft-orange flowers have orange beards. Very early to mid. **H** 46cm (MTB)

'Az Ap' (Ensminger 1979) Neat, sky-blue flowers, lightly flecked with purple and with bushy, bright-blue beards, bloom over a long period. Early to late. **H** 56cm (IB)

'Baby Blessed' (Zurbrigg 1979) The pretty, soft-yellow flowers have ruffled, rounded standards and falls that are striped with white either side of the pale-lemon beards. Early. Remontant. **H** 25cm (SDB)

'Bangles' (Miller 1993) A petite flower with rounded, rosy-lavender standards and flaring, deep violet-veined, lavender-blue falls. The white beards are brushed with yellow. Early to late. H 53cm (MTB)

'Bluebeard's Ghost' (Black 2006) This delightful and special plant has lightly scented, milky-white flowers with very conspicuous bright-blue beards. Early to late. **H** 37cm (SDB)

'Bronzaire' (Bartlett 1991) A smooth, bronze-yellow flower with bushy, soft-ginger beards, ruffled standards, and wavy, velvety falls. Early to mid. **H** 51cm (IB)

Iris 'Apricot Drops'

Iris 'Az Ap'

Iris 'Baby Blessed'

Iris 'Bangles'

Iris 'Bluebeard's Ghost'

Iris 'Bronzaire'

Iris 'Bumblebee Deelite'

Iris 'Chubby Cheeks'

'Bumblebee Deelite' (Norrick 1985) These dinky flowers with flaring, yellow-rimmed, black-maroon falls and short, yellow standards are a real delight. The blooms are carried on slender stems above bright green leaves. Early to mid. **H** 46cm (MTB)

'Chanted' (Blyth 1991) Used extensively to raise plants with pink-toned flowers, this Australian iris has strongly scented, dusky apricot-pink flowers with pale-blue beards. Mid. **H** 34cm (SDB)

'Chubby Cheeks' (P. Black 1984) Small and scented, the soft violet-speckled, white flowers have rather crumpled, rounded petals and bronze-tipped, soft-violet beards. The parent of many standard dwarf bearded irises with evenly sized, rounded petals. Early. **H** 30cm (SDB)

'Dividing Line' (Bunnell 2004) The first MTB iris to be awarded the prestigious Dykes medal. The slender stems are topped with small, soft rosy-purple flowers. The falls have a large, dark rosy-purple spot and white veins around the yellow beards. Dykes 2014. Mid. **H** 56cm (MTB)

'Enriched' (Craig 2000) Delicate, perfectly symmetrical standards of soft lemon and very pale, almost watercolour-washed, lilac falls are borne on slim stems. Early to mid. **H** 58cm (MTB)

'Eramosa Skies' (Chapman 1996) Raised in Canada, this tough plant has violet-blue petals and beards. Mid. **H** 33cm (SDB)

'Fathom' (Smith 1996) I love this flower simply because its rich sky-blue petals are so thick and smooth. The beards are a matching blue. Mid to late. **H** 58cm (IB)

Iris 'Chanted'

Iris 'Dividing Line'

Iris 'Enriched'

Iris 'Eramosa Skies'

Iris 'Fathom'

'Forever Blue' (Chapman 1996) This never fails to bloom again in August with soft grey-blue flowers. There are green patches on the falls and bright-blue, V-shaped beards. Early. Remontant. **H** 30cm (SDB)

'Heather Carpet' (Chapman 1999) For rich, intense colour, this iris is hard to beat. The large flowers are a sparkling, rosy-purple shade with large, bushy, white beards. Mid. **H** 30cm (SDB)

'Headline Banner' (Sutton 1998) The large, strongly scented, smoky-violet flowers have a white patch on the falls that is speckled with white and edged with ochre. Mid to late. **H** 66cm (BB)

'Just Jennifer' (Taylor 1983) A lovely plant with perfectly proportioned, gently ruffled, pure-white flowers. There are not many short irises as robust as this one. Early. **H** 64cm (BB)

'Lemon Pop' (Lauer 1989) This lightly ruffled, scented, soft-yellow variety has white patches on the falls. The thick, white beards are tipped with yellow towards the back. Early. **H** 41cm (IB)

'Lilli-white' (Welch 1957) The first white standard dwarf bearded iris to be bred, and still a good variety. It has pure-white flowers with white beards. Late. **H** 30cm (SDB)

'Maid of Orange' (Aitken 1989) Orange-flowered irises are never as tough as those in other colours, but this is reasonably robust. It has gently ruffled, orange flowers with vivid-orange beards and a light, fruity scent. Early to late. **H** 64cm (BB)

Iris 'Forever Blue'

Iris 'Heather Carpet'

Iris 'Headline Banner'

Iris 'Just Jennifer'

Iris 'Lemon Pop'

Iris 'Lilli-white'

Iris 'Maid of Orange'

Iris 'New Idea'

Iris 'Orinoco Flow'

Iris 'Panther'

Iris 'Pause'

Iris 'Peebee and Jay'

Iris 'Pussycat Pink'

Iris 'Prairie Thunder'

'New Idea' (Hager 1970) The small rosy-mauve flowers feature a smear of violet on the falls, which enhances their smooth form. In damp summers this will bloom a second time. Early to mid. **H** 26cm (MTB)

'Orinoco Flow' (Bartlett 1989) The only border bearded iris to have won the Dykes medal in the UK. This has very ruffled, heavily scented, white flowers that are beautifully edged with bands of violet-blue 'stitching'. The beards are blue. Dykes 1994. Early to late. **H** 64cm (BB)

'Panther' (Smith 2002) A delightful purple-black variety with crumpled, flaring falls, wide-open standards, and bushy, violet beards. Early to mid. **H** 30cm (SDB)

'Pause' (Blyth 2001) The unusual, sweetly scented flowers have delicate, soft-pink standards, violet falls, and tangerine-tipped, violet beards. Early to mid. **H** 30cm (SDB)

'Peebee and Jay' (Schmieder 2005) The flowers may be small, but the colour is vibrant. Rounded, caramel standards touch at the top, and the flaring, rose-violet falls are also rimmed with caramel. The beards are yellow. Mid. **H** 26cm (MTB)

'Pussycat Pink' (Black 2006) Perfectly shaped, the flowers are an incredibly bright shade of hot pink with bright-coral beards. Mid to late. **H** 30cm (SDB)

'Prairie Thunder' (Johnson 1990) This Arilbred iris (AB) is the result of a cross between a desert-dwelling Aril iris and an intermediate bearded iris. A robust plant, it has exotic flowers with soft violet-blue standards, greyish-buff falls with a maroon flare, and bronze-tipped, blue beards. Mid. **H** 64cm

'Princess Bride' (Sutton 1999) Pretty and ruffled, the creamy-white flowers are carried on strong stems. They have bushy, deep orange-yellow beards and big, thick petals. Mid to very late. **H** 64cm (BB)

'Riveting' (Black 2009) Strongly scented, pure-white flowers have open standards and flaring falls that are partly covered by a large, ink-blue spot. The beards are white. Mid to late. **H** 38cm (SDB)

'Ruby Eruption' (Chapman 1997) A scented, heavily ruffled, dark rose-purple iris. The flower colour is stippled over a yellow background, around the red-tipped, cream beards. Mid to late. **H** 30cm (SDB)

'Star in the Night' (Black 2009) Handsome and neatly ruffled, the scented flowers have dark inky-blue standards and smooth, velvety, blue-black falls. The broad, soft-blue beards are touched with yellow. Mid to late. **H** 64cm (IB)

'Starwoman' (Smith 1998) A lovely plant with thick, silky, scented, blue-purple flowers. The flaring, wavy falls are heavily smeared with white below the yellow-brushed, soft-blue beards. Dykes 2008. Mid. **H** 64cm (IB)

'Ultimate' (Johnson 2002) A gloriously cheerful plant with large, primrose-yellow flowers. The yellow-rimmed falls are almost entirely deep brown and the sparse beards are also yellow. Mid. **H** 33cm (SDB)

'Yippy Skippy' (Black 1998) A delightful iris with rosy-purple flowers. The creamy-white background colour of the petals is revealed when you look inside. This tough little doer produces one or two flowers in autumn. Mid. **H** 30cm (SDB)

Iris 'Princess Bride'

Iris 'Riveting'

Iris 'Ruby Eruption'

Iris 'Star in the Night'

Iris 'Starwoman'

Iris 'Ultimate'

Iris 'Yippy Skippy'

SIBIRICA IRISES

These are supremely graceful plants. The flowers are carried towards the top of tall, slender stems above upright clumps of slim, grassy foliage. Siberian irises are tolerant of many conditions: partial shade to full sun; dry spots – although they take longer to establish – to really wet and even quite acid soils. Some are a little more fussy; their preferences are given in the description.

Flowering These bloom around early, mid- or late June, at the same time as tall bearded irises.

'Butter and Sugar' (McEwen 1976) This was the first non-fading yellow and white Sibirica iris. The slender, white standards have green-yellow veins, and the rounded falls are soft yellow. Mid. **H** 68cm

'Caesar's Brother' (Cleveland Morgan 1932) Still popular, the flowers of this long-established iris are rich blue-purple with short, yellow and white signals on each fall. The standards flare outwards above the broad, twisting falls. Mid. **H** 99cm

'Careless Sally' (Schafer/Sacks '96) The flowers are flatter than is usual for the Siberian iris. Gently ruffled, the soft-lilac falls are rounded and splashed with rosy-lilac. They sit below flaring, pale lilac-white standards. Mid. **H** 66cm

chrysographes This iris likes a moist, acidic soil. The small, deep purple-black flowers, brushed with short stripes of golden-yellow on the falls, are carried in ones and twos on slender stems above very upright, slim, mid-green leaves. Late. **H** 45cm

'Flight of Butterflies' (Witt 1972) A delicate flower with violet-blue standards and white falls so heavily patterned with violet-blue they resemble butterfly wings. The small blooms are carried on long, slender stems. Mid. **H** 91cm

forrestii This pretty species has scented, soft-yellow flowers with broken lines of brown-purple on the oval falls. The standards are upright. The glossy, green leaves have grey-green backs. Early to mid. **H** 75cm

Iris 'Butter and Sugar'

Iris 'Caesar's Brother'

Iris 'Careless Sally'

Iris chrysographes

Iris 'Flight of Butterflies'

Iris forrestii

'Peter Hewitt' (Hewitt 2003) A striking flower with deep blue-violet falls, finely edged with gold, and gold signals. The violet-blue standards have darker veins. Dykes UK 2008. Mid to late. **H** 94cm.

'Roaring Jelly' (Schafer/Sacks 1992) Rounded and red-purple in colour, the falls have a circle of gold veins towards the top. The soft reddish-purple standards display deeper-coloured veins. Mid. **H** 90cm

'Ruffles and Flourishes' (Hollingsworth 2002) An award-winning variety with broad, rosy-purple petals. The rounded, ruffled falls are edged in white, which also extends out from the golden flare. A lovely big flower this sits well above the leaves. Mid to late. **H** 90cm

'Salamander Crossing' (Schafer/Sacks 1999) Delicate and rather dignified, the flowers have rounded, soft-yellow falls, finely spotted and veined with lilac. Speckles of the same colour cover the white standards. Early to late. **H** 107cm

'Silver Edge' (McEwen 1973) The petals of the elegant, mid-blue flowers are finely rimmed with white and gently ruffled. Early to mid. **H** 71cm

'Sparkling Rose' (Hager 1967) These flowers really do sparkle. They open out flat and are a bright rose-mauve shade, flushed with blue. Mid. **H** 97cm

'White Swirl' (Cassebeer 1957) A pretty pure-white flower with gently ruffled, flaring petals. This important introduction was the first Siberian iris with falls that flared outwards. The base of the petals is golden-yellow. Late. **H** 102cm

Iris 'Peter Hewitt'

Iris 'Roaring Jelly'

Iris 'Ruffles and Flourishes'

Iris 'Salamander Crossing'

Iris 'Silver Edge'

Iris 'Sparkling Rose'

Iris 'White Swirl'

Iris 'Ally Oops'

Iris ensata

Iris foetidissima

Iris 'Holden's Child'

Iris pseudacorus

Iris × *robusta* 'Gerald Darby'

These irises grow happily in moist soils, although only Iris pseudacorus *will actually grow in water.* I. foetidissima *and* I. setosa *will also tolerate dry soils. All flower from early to late June.*

'Ally Oops' (Borglum 2002) This tall, elegant iris carries its exquisite flowers in twos or threes high above a wide clump of mid-green leaves. The tiny standards are lilac and the large, rounded, soft-lemon falls are traced with lilac veins. Thought to be a cross between a Siberian iris and *I. pseudacorus*. Mid to late. **H** 75cm

ensata (Japanese iris) This is a big group, but the choice of garden-worthy varieties is very limited. All the flower petals lie flat, curling softly around the edges. The colours vary from soft lilac and white to dark purple, and all have yellow flashes on the falls. This iris won't grow in water for long and prefers the margins of ponds or very moist soil. Usually grown from seed. Late. **H** 90cm

foetidissima Valued for its leaves and berries, rather than the flowers, this robust iris will grow in any soil in sun or shade. The upright clump of deep-green leaves is evergreen and short stems of yellowish-brown flowers turn into bright orange-red seeds in autumn. Mid. **H** 45cm

'Holden's Child' (Tiffney 1988) Great for a wet soil, and even a spot with little light. The flowers have very short, lilac standards and the purple falls, which have gold and white signals, look like dog's ears. A vigorous plant, its broad, mid-green leaves form a thick, bushy clump. Early to late. **H** 76cm

pseudacorus (Yellow flag) Rising from a dense clump of mid-green leaves, tall, well-branched stems carry bright-yellow flowers. The falls usually, but not always, have dark brown markings and the standards are spoon-shaped. Useful for growing in bogs or large pools, it will tolerate most conditions, even well-drained, sandy soil. Early to late. **H** 120cm

× *robusta* 'Gerald Darby' (Coe-Darby 1968) I would grow this just for the long, purple-tinted stems that emerge from a vigorous, broad clump of wide, deep-green leaves. Later, violet-blue flowers appear in clusters over a long period. Early to late. **H** 76cm

setosa In the wild, this is the most widely distributed iris, adapting to wet and dry soils alike. The soft-blue flowers have flaring, short standards; the falls are rounded and marked with yellowish-white and purple. The broad, arching leaves grow into a thick clump. Largely grown from seed, so colours and heights may vary. Early to late. **H** 45–75cm

Iris setosa

Iris unguicularis

Iris Pacific Coast Hybrid

Iris 'Betty Cooper'

Iris 'Lucky Devil'

Iris 'Media Luz'

unguicularis Evergreen and winter-flowering, this iris has scented, rich-lavender flowers that sit deep within a broad clump of deep green, narrow foliage. It prefers a dry soil in sun and can be slow to establish. December–February. **H** 60cm

PACIFIC COAST IRISES
These low-growing irises need to be grown in acid soil. Resenting disturbance, they are usually grown from seed, which is not difficult. The delicious flowers have flat, broad petals ranging in colour from white to dark red, yellow, and blue. They are borne in sprays on long stems that spring up from a broad, low mound of slender, deep-green, evergreen leaves. Late. **H** 30cm

SPURIA IRISES
The flowers of these tall plants are similar to those of bulbous Dutch irises, and are carried up stiff stems above a dense clump of tall, deep-green leaves. They are the last of the summer-flowering irises to bloom, the flowers are great for cutting, and also loved by bees. Spuria irises thrive anywhere, but establish faster in moist soils. Flowering time is late June to early July.

'Betty Cooper' (McCown 1981) This iris has frilly, soft-lilac flowers with a large, yellow-orange spot on the falls. Mid. **H** 123cm

'Lucky Devil' (Ghio 1987) The broad, deep-purple flowers are washed with magenta and the falls are stained with yellow. Early to mid. **H** 91cm

'Media Luz' (Hager 1967) A pretty shade of soft lavender, the falls are tinged with cream and have yellow signals. Late. **H** 101cm

'Missouri Autumn' (Niswonger 1996) The burnt-orange flowers darken to a coppery-brown at the edges. Mid. **H** 102cm

Iris 'Missouri Autumn'

Kirengeshoma palmata

Knautia macedonica

Kniphofia 'Alcazar'

Kniphofia 'Brimstone'

Kniphofia 'Nobilis'

Kniphofia 'Toffee Nosed'

KIRENGESHOMA

palmata This lovely, unusual, woodland plant sends up sprays of waxy, shuttlecock-like, soft-yellow flowers on long stems. Its maple-like, soft-green leaves form an open clump. August to September. **H × S** 120cm × 75cm.

Needs Well-drained, humus-rich soil that remains moist in partial shade
Great for Woodlands and damp soils
Bees & Butterflies No
For Cutting No
Care Slow to establish. Protect from slugs

KNAUTIA

macedonica A must for the wildlife garden. Masses of scabious-like, blue-crimson flowers top a spindly network of well-branched stems with soft-green leaves. June to August. **H × S** 80cm × 60cm

Needs Well-drained soil in sun or partial shade
Great for Front or middle of the border
Bees & Butterflies Yes
For Cutting Yes
Care Easy to grow. Seeds freely about

KNIPHOFIA (Red-hot poker)

Upright and stately, these bold plants carry fat spikes of long, tubular flowers. They are held on cylindrical stems high above a rosette of rush-like, evergreen usually mid-green leaves. Opening from the base of the spike first, the buds frequently vary in colour from the open blooms.

Needs Really well-drained soil in sun
Great for Vertical structure in the border
Bees & Butterflies Bees
For Cutting Yes
Care Will not thrive in soils that stay wet during winter

'Alcazar' An easily established, free-flowering variety with flaming-red spikes opening from bright-yellow buds. June to September. **H × S** 105cm × 60cm

'Brimstone' Late to flower, its yellow pokers open from lime-green buds on bronze-tinted stems with slender leaves. August to October. **H × S** 75cm × 60cm. AGM

'Nobilis' This handsome plant has fat spikes of eye-catching, bright-red flowers that open from yellow buds. July to October. **H × S** 120cm × 90cm

'Toffee Nosed' Loose spikes of soft-orange flowers carried on bronze stems open from cream buds. July to October. **H × S** 90cm × 60cm. AGM

LAMIUM (Deadnettle)

Most deadnettles make ideal ground-cover and all have leafy stems with whorls of small, hooded flowers and heart-shaped, jagged-edged, often decorative leaves. *Lamium orvala* forms an upright mound.

Needs Well-drained soil in sun, partial shade, or full shade
Great for Front of the border and woodland
Bees & Butterflies Bees
For Cutting No
Care Most are easy to grow, although *L. orvala* may take a while to establish

galeobdolon **'Florentinum'** (Yellow archangel) A vigorous plant and ideal for ground-cover in damp shade. Produces long, creeping stems of silver-splashed, heart-shaped leaves and yellow flowers. May to June. **H × S** 45cm × 75cm

maculatum **'White Nancy'** A low, carpeting plant with pure-white flowers rising from mid-green leaves that are coated almost entirely with silver. May to June. **H × S** 15cm × 30cm

orvala (Great deadnettle) Unlike the others in the group, this grows into a handsome, upright plant. Stiff stems of large, velvety, soft-purple flowers emerge between big, mid-green leaves. May to June. **H × S** 45cm × 45cm

LAMPROCAPNOS (Bleeding heart)

Still found under their old name *Dicentra*, these most graceful spring plants have large, locket-shaped flowers, each with a drooping, white teardrop. They dangle in a row from long, arching stems that emerge from a dense, upright clump of succulent, but soft, deeply divided leaves.

Needs Well-drained soil that remains moist in partial or full shade
Great for Wooded and shady spots
Bees & Butterflies No
For Cutting No
Care They die back entirely by midsummer

spectabilis Pure-pink flowers hang from thick, upright, red-tinted stems with lush, deeply divided, mid-green leaves. April to June. **H × S** 60cm × 50cm. AGM

spectabilis **'Alba'** Beautiful when fully established, this variety has pure-white flowers and fresh-green leaves. April to June. **H × S** 60cm × 50cm. AGM

spectabilis **'Valentine'** A wonderful, fairly recent addition to the clan. The vermilion-red flowers dangle along purple-tinged stems above deeply divided, green leaves tinted with maroon. April to June. **H × S** 60cm × 50cm

Lamium galeobdolon 'Florentinum'

Lamium maculatum 'White Nancy'

Lamium orvala

Lamprocapnos spectabilis

Lamprocapnos spectabilis 'Alba'

Lamprocapnos spectabilis 'Valentine'

Lathyrus latifolius 'Rosa Perle'

Lathyrus vernus

Leucanthemella serotina

Leucanthemum × *superbum* 'Aglaia'

Leucanthemum × *superbum* 'Becky'

LATHYRUS (Everlasting pea)

There are two types of perennial sweet pea: those that ramble and early-flowering clump-forming types. Neither is scented, but the flowers are distinctly pea-like.

Needs Well-drained soil in sun or partial shade
Great for Front of the border or let them scramble through other plants
Bees & Butterflies No
For Cutting No
Care Remove seedheads if you don't want seedlings around the garden

***latifolius* 'Rosa Perle'** (Perennial sweet pea) A non-clinging, free-flowering climber with large, pink blooms carried up leafy stems that will ramble over a wall, a hedge, or down a bank. Usually raised from seed so colours may vary. The pure-white form is usually sold as *L. latifolius* 'White Pearl'. June to September. **H × S** 150cm × 75cm. AGM

vernus One of the very first perennials to bloom, it flowers before the leaves appear. Masses of slender stems unfurl into sprays of small, vibrant-purple flowers. The long, pointed, deep-green leaves eventually form a neat clump. Colours can vary: the pink-flowered form is known as *L. vernus* 'Alboroseus'. March to May. **H × S** 30cm × 30cm. AGM

LEUCANTHEMELLA

serotina A very late-flowering daisy with sprays of large, pure-white blooms on leafy branches towards the top of the tall stems. These are the only daisy-shaped perennials to turn their heads to face the sun, like sunflowers. September to October. **H × S** 150cm × 90cm. AGM

Needs Well-drained soil that retains its moisture, in sun or partial shade
Great for Very back of the border
Bees & Butterflies Yes
For Cutting Yes
Care Trouble free and needs no staking

LEUCANTHEMUM (Shasta daisy)

Once listed as *Chrysanthemum superbum*, only white forms of this perennial were available. Now yellow varieties have been bred. The large, daisy flowers are carried on stiff stems with no branches above a thick clump of semi-evergreen, long, mid-green leaves. They form broad clumps.

Needs Well-drained soil in full sun
Great for Front and middle of the border
Bees & Butterflies Yes
For Cutting Yes
Care Trouble free

× superbum 'Aglaia' Large, white blooms with shorter, central petals give this double 'frilly' form a distinctly shaggy look. June to August. **H × S** 90cm × 60cm

× superbum 'Becky' A clean plant with single, sometimes semi-double, white flowers that form a neat, round clump. June to August. **H × S** 90cm × 60cm

× superbum 'Broadway Lights' Stems of single, primrose-yellow flowers fade to cream on this compact plant, creating a two-tone effect. June to August. **H × S** 50cm × 45cm

× superbum 'Engelina' A short plant with fully double, white flowers made up of slender petals. These are so thick and fluffy that the heads look rather like poached eggs. June to August. **H × S** 50cm × 50cm

× superbum 'Phyllis Smith' Carries very frilly, single, white flowers on stiff, stems that support themselves well. June to August. **H × S** 90cm × 75cm

× superbum 'Sonnenschein' The single flowers have soft-yellow petals that unfurl around a golden centre. They are carried on stems that can, however, be rather floppy. Very effective when planted in drifts. June to August. **H × S** 90cm × 75cm

× superbum 'T. E. Killin' An old variety with smooth, white outer petals and a further ring of shorter inner ones encircling a golden centre. June to August. **H × S** 90cm × 75cm. AGM

× superbum 'Wirral Supreme' White flowers with a flat, yellow disc are edged with rows of short petals. These extend over almost the whole centre of this double form. June to August. **H × S** 50cm × 45cm. AGM

Leucanthemum × superbum 'Broadway Lights'

Leucanthemum × superbum 'Engelina'

Leucanthemum × superbum 'Phyllis Smith'

Leucanthemum × superbum 'T. E. Killin'

Leucanthemum × superbum 'Sonnenschein'

Leucanthemum × superbum 'Wirral Supreme'

Liatris spicata

Ligularia dentata 'Othello'

Limonium platyphyllum

Ligularia przewalskii

LIATRIS (Gayfeather)

spicata More often seen in flower arrangements than in gardens, this plant is very easy to grow. Slender spikes of small, fluffy, rich-lilac flowers open from the top first. They are carried on strong stems that rise from a tuft of slim leaves. August to September. **H × S** 75cm × 45cm

Needs Well-drained soil, including very light soil that retains moisture in summer
Great for Middle of the border
Bees & Butterflies Yes
For Cutting Yes
Care Dig up and split the clumps every few years to keep the plant vigorous.

LIGULARIA

These bold plants are ideal for gardens with damp soil. All produce yellow daisies in clusters or elegant spires, but the foliage is what makes the plants stand out. The leaves are big, some are round, and the most decorative are deeply divided into fingers.

Needs Soil that remains damp in sun, partial shade, or shade
Great for Very damp or wet ground
Bees & Butterflies Yes
For Cutting Yes
Care Does not thrive in dry or light soils

dentata **'Othello'** Sprays of big yellow daisies on branched stems sit high above rounded, deep purple-green leaves that are the colour of red wine underneath. July to August. **H × S** 90cm × 75cm

przewalskii This graceful plant carries its tapering spikes of small, star-like, golden flowers on black stems above a mound of large, deeply divided, mid-green leaves. July to August. **H × S** 105cm × 75cm

LIMONIUM (Sea lavender)

platyphyllum A haze of tiny, papery, lavender flowers hovers over slender, well-branched, almost woody stems. These spring from a rosette of long, leathery, mid-green leaves. August to September. **H × S** 45cm × 45cm

Needs Well-drained soil, including dry, in sun
Great for Front of the border
Bees & Butterflies Yes
For Cutting Yes
Care Good for seaside gardens

LINARIA (Toadflax)

These elegant and generous plants bear slender spikes of tiny flowers, shaped like miniature snapdragons. The upright stems with slim leaves need no support. Self-seeds freely around the garden.

Needs Well-drained soil in sun or partial shade
Great for Anywhere in the border
Bees & Butterflies Bees
For Cutting Yes
Care Deadhead promptly if you don't want lots of seedlings

purpurea This variety has tiny, rich-purple flowers and mid-green leaves. July to October. **H × S** 90cm × 45cm

purpurea **'Canon Went'** Spikes of small, pink flowers are carried above the grey leaves. July to October. **H × S** 90cm × 45cm

LIRIOPE (Lily turf)

muscari An evergreen plant with grass-like, mid-green leaves that forms arching tufts. These creep along the ground and send up dark-maroon stems with tight spikes of bud-like, bright-violet flowers. July to October. **H × S** 45cm × 45cm. AGM

Needs Well-drained soil in sun to dappled shade
Great for Front of the border
Bees & Butterflies Bees
For Cutting No
Care Best in a shady spot as the flower colour can fade in strong sunlight

LOBELIA

siphilitica All lobelias love moist soil and are easily grown from seed, but they can be tricky to keep perennial. This variety has spikes of large-lipped flowers in a deep shade of sky-blue. The lush, mid-green leaves grow into a handsome clump. July to September. **H × S** 90cm × 45cm. AGM

Needs Soil that does not dry out
Great for Bog gardens and around ponds, in sun or partial shade
Bees & Butterflies Yes
For Cutting No
Care Lobelias can be rather short-lived

LUNARIA (Honesty)

rediviva This rather demure but desirable perennial form of honesty is not always easy to grow. An upright plant, it produces clusters of small, scented, palest-lilac flowers over a long period. Translucent, oval seed pods follow. Deep-green, heart-shaped leaves are carried right up the stiff stems. June to August. **H × S** 90cm × 45cm. AGM

Needs Well-drained soil in sun or partial shade; best in a rich soil
Great for Middle of the border
Bees & Butterflies Yes
For Cutting Yes
Care Slow to get established, otherwise trouble free

Linaria purpurea

Lobelia siphilitica

Linaria purpurea 'Canon Went'

Liriope muscari

Lunaria rediviva

Lupinus 'Chandelier'

Lupinus 'Noble Maiden'

Lupinus 'Persian Slipper' with
Sanguisorba menziesii

Lupinus 'The Chatelaine'

Lupinus 'The Governor'

LUPINUS (Lupin)

These big, colourful plants send up their stately spires just as many spring flowers are fading. Tightly packed with large, pea-shaped flowers, they are carried above a shapely mound of deeply fingered, mid-green leaves.

Needs Well-drained soil in sun
Great for Middle to back of the border
Bees & Butterflies No
For Cutting Yes, but they have hollow stems and can wilt quickly.
Care Remove flowers before they go to seed to maintain vigour. Slugs can be a problem

'Chandelier' The flower colour of this seed-raised variety can range from soft- to mid-yellow. May to June. **H × S** 90cm × 80cm

'Noble Maiden' A seed-raised plant with flowers in shades from pure white to palest cream. May to June. **H × S** 90cm × 80cm

'Persian Slipper' One of a new breed of short lupins with tight spikes of purple-blue flowers. Usually raised from stock plants rather than seed, so will not vary in colour. May to June. **H × S** 60cm × 50cm

'The Chatelaine' Flowers are usually salmon-pink with white lower petals, although the spikes are sometimes entirely pink. May to June. **H × S** 90cm × 80cm

'The Governor' On this variable, seed-raised plant, the flowers are usually deep-blue and white, but the lower petals can be lilac. May to June. **H × S** 90cm × 80cm

LYCHNIS (Campion)

Cheerful and prolific, these quick-growing plants have flat, open flowers on upright, well-branched stems.

Needs Well-drained soil in sun or partial shade
Great for Middle and back of the border
Bees & Butterflies Yes
For Cutting Yes (*L. chalcedonica*)
Care Trouble free but short-lived

chalcedonica (Maltese cross) Small, vivid-scarlet flowers sit in clusters on upright, bright-green stems that can be weak in the first year, but strengthen in the second. June to August. **H × S** 90cm × 60cm. AGM

coronaria (Dusty miller) A network of stiff, grey stems is topped with flat, strikingly coloured flowers in deep cerise. The woolly, grey leaves form a tight, upright clump. June to August. **H × S** 75cm × 60cm. AGM

coronaria **'Alba'** This cool, white form of dusty miller has soft, silvery foliage. The flowers bloom over a long period. June to August. **H × S** 75cm × 60cm. AGM

Lychnis chalcedonica
with *Campanula lactiflora* behind

Lychnis coronaria 'Alba'

Lychnis coronaria with spikes of *Salvia nemorosa* 'Amethyst' with lavender-blue
Nepeta 'Six Hills Giant' behind

Lysimachia ciliata 'Firecracker'

Lysimachia ephemerum

Lysimachia punctata

Lysimachia punctata 'Alexander'

Lythrum salicaria 'Blush'

Lythrum salicaria 'Robert'

LYSIMACHIA (Loosestrife)

In early spring the newly emerging stems of these attractive perennials add interest to the garden. As the season progresses, they form an upright, broad clump with spires of starry flowers.

Needs Soil that remains moist in sun or partial shade
Great for Middle of the border
Bees & Butterflies Yes
For Cutting Yes
Care Vigorous, so more suited to bigger gardens

ciliata **'Firecracker'** This eye-catching plant has stems of long, pointed, mahogany leaves. Loose clusters of small, yellow flowers spring from each leaf joint. June to August. **H × S** 90cm × 90cm. AGM

clethroides A bushy plant with red stems bearing spikes of tiny, white flowers that arch gracefully forward. June to August. **H × S** 90cm × 90cm. AGM

ephemerum This elegant, rigidly, upright plant has slender spikes of tiny, starry, white flowers. The stems and leaves are waxy, grey-green stems. June to August. **H × S** 90cm × 75cm. AGM

punctata A vigorous, spreading plant that will easily romp, filling a border quickly with tall stems of cupped, starry, yellow flowers opening between bright-green leaves. June to August. **H × S** 90cm × 90cm

punctata **'Alexander'** Like the one above, but much more decorative with slightly ruffled, cream-edged, soft-green leaves and spikes of yellow, cupped flowers. Not quite as vigorous. June to August. **H × S** 90cm × 90cm

LYTHRUM (Purple loosestrife)

These are garden hybrids of our native plant, which is found along streams. The flowers have rather unruly petals and form slender, tapering spikes above a strong, upright clump of slim, mid-green leaves.

Needs Soil that remains moist in sun or partial shade
Great for Middle of the border
Bees & Butterflies Yes
For Cutting Yes
Care Damp soils

salicaria **'Blush'** A pretty plant with long, tapering spikes of soft-pink flowers. Mid-green leaves colour in autumn. June to August. **H × S** 90cm × 75cm. AGM

salicaria **'Robert'** A short plant with spikes of rich-pink flowers and mid-green leaves. June to August. **H × S** 60cm × 45cm

Lysimachia clethroides with the yellow and red *Helenium* 'Sahin's Early Flowerer' backed by *Eupatorium maculatum* 'Riesenschirm'

Macleaya microcarpa

Meconopsis × sheldonii

Melittis melissophyllum

Mertensia virginica

Milium effusum 'Aureum'

MACLEAYA (Plume poppy)

microcarpa This lofty plant produces tall, slender stems that end in wispy, feathery plumes of tiny, buff-pink flowers. Handsome, fig-shaped, blue-green leaves stand out horizontally towards the bottom of the stems and at the base. July to August. **H × S** 180cm × 105cm. AGM

Needs Well-drained soil in sun or partial shade
Great for Back of a big border
Bees & Butterflies Bees
For Cutting No
Care Can become invasive If it likes the spot

MECONOPSIS

× sheldonii On this stunning, rather choosy plant, vivid violet-blue, cupped flowers nod elegantly in clusters on tall, hairy stems above a rosette of long, mid-green leaves. A very similar plant, *M. betonicifolia*, has lovely sky-blue flowers followed by slender seed pods. July to August. **H × S** 120cm × 45cm

Needs Moist soil, preferably with lots of leafmould, in partial or full shade
Great for Areas with shade cast by trees
Bees & Butterflies Bees
For Cutting No
Care The great plantsman Graham Stuart Thomas advised me to remove the first flower buds before they bloom to get a better show the following year. For some reason, I never like to do this.

MELITTIS (Bastard balm)

melissophyllum I first saw this growing wild in a woodland in Devon. An upright plant with large, white, magenta-lipped flowers that spring from the stem above each pair of leaves. June to August. **H × S** 60cm × 50cm

Needs Soil that remains moist in partial shade
Great for Shady areas including woodland
Bees & Butterflies Yes
For Cutting Yes
Care May take a little while to establish, but trouble free

MERTENSIA (Virginia cowslip)

virginica On this pretty, slowly spreading plant loose clusters of trumpet-shaped, sky-blue flowers are held on waxy stems with oval, blue-green leaves. April to May. **H × S** 45cm × 45cm. AGM

Needs Reliably moist soil in partial shade
Great for Dappled shade
Bees & Butterflies No
For Cutting No
Care Tricky to grow and can attract slugs

MILIUM

effusum 'Aureum' (Bowles's golden grass)
A useful semi-evergreen grass. In spring, the new leaves are yellow, deepening to soft green by summer. The slender flower spikes are yellow. July. **H × S** 45cm × 50cm. AGM

Needs Soil that does not dry out in sun or partial shade
Great for Front of the border
Bees & Butterflies No
For Cutting No
Care Liable to seed around

MISCANTHUS (Silver grass)

Handsome and clump-forming, these upright grasses have slim, straight leaves and tall stems topped with plumes of very small, silky flowers in strands, like fly whisks. They are very hardy, long-lived, and ideal tall grasses for a border.

Needs Well-drained soil in sun or partial shade
Great for Back of the border
Bees & Butterflies No
For Cutting No
Care Cut the old leaves back in spring

sinensis 'Flamingo' Arching plumes of tan-pink flowers rise from mid-green leaves with good autumn colour. August to September. **H × S** 120cm × 75cm. AGM

sinensis 'Morning Light' A plant to lighten up a border, with silver-edged leaves and fluffy flowers that fade to silver. August to September. **H × S** 120cm × 75cm. AGM

sinensis 'Silberfeder' Plumes of silver-pink flowers are reliably produced from a thick clump of mid-green leaves. August to September. **H × S** 180cm × 75cm. AGM

sinensis 'Zebrinus' From mid-green leaves with distinctive, yellow bands rise tall stems topped with plumes of silver-buff flowers. September. **H × S** 180cm × 90cm. AGM

MOLINIA (Moor grass)

caerulea subsp. caerulea 'Strahlenquelle'
This lovely 'see-through' grass produces a broad tuft of slender, mid-green leaves that turn gold in autumn. In late summer sprays of soft-purple flowers erupt turning soft brown as they age. August to September. **H × S** 90cm × 60cm

Needs Soil that remains moist in sun or partial shade
Great for Anywhere in the border where light can shine through
Bees & Butterflies No
For Cutting No
Care Not invasive and trouble free

Miscanthus sinensis 'Flamingo'

Miscanthus sinensis 'Morning Light'

Miscanthus sinensis 'Zebrinus'

Miscanthus sinensis *'Silberfeder'*

Molinia caerulea subsp. *caerulea* 'Strahlenquelle'

Monarda 'Beauty of Cobham'

Monarda 'Fireball'

Monarda 'Cambridge Scarlet'

MONARDA (Bergamot)

Noted for their bright colours, bergamot flowers also attract bees. The stiff stems are crowned by long-lipped, tubular flowers on top of coloured bracts, and the plant forms a handsome, upright clump that needs no staking. When crushed, the mid-green leaves exude a distinctive, pleasant scent.

Needs Well-drained soil that remains moist in sun or partial shade
Great for Middle of the border
Bees & Butterflies Bees
For Cutting Yes
Care Can be prone to mildew, especially if the soil dries out

'Beauty of Cobham' A pretty, clump-forming plant with soft-pink flowers sitting on rosy-purple bracts. June to August. H × S 90cm × 60cm. AGM

'Cambridge Scarlet' On this showy variety, dark red bracts are topped with bright-scarlet flowers. June to August. H × S 90cm × 60cm.

'Fireball' Useful for the front of the border, this stocky plant bears rich-red flowers with purple-stained bracts. June to August. H × S 60cm × 40cm

'Prärienacht' A free-flowering plant. The whorls of rosy-purple blooms sit on green bracts. June to August. H × S 90cm × 60cm

'Schneewittchen' Named after fairytale heroine Snow White, this variety has pure-white flowers with green bracts. June to August. H × S 90cm × 60cm

'Scorpion' Flowering a little later than the others, this variety has rosy-purple flowers and purple bracts. June to August. H × S 90cm × 60cm

Monarda 'Prärienacht'

Monarda 'Schneewittchen'

Monarda 'Scorpion'

MORINA

longifolia An intriguing and curious plant that may appear a bit too thistle-like for some. The long, drooping, white flowers emerge from a spiky, cup-like collar and are carried in whorls up the strong stems. As the flowers age, they are touched with pink. At the base of the plant the long, spiky, leathery, fresh-green leaves form an evergreen rosette. July to August. **H × S** 60cm × 30cm.

Needs Well-drained soil in sun
Great for Edge of the border alongside ground-covering plants
Bees & Butterflies Bees
For Cutting No
Care May take a year or two to develop

NEPETA (Catmint)

Invaluable for mixing with other perennials, catmints are also useful for filling a border quickly. Many produce frothy stems of small, large-lipped flowers above a bushy clump of soft-green leaves, which are aromatic when crushed. More upright varieties are ideal for the back of a border.

Needs Well-drained soil in sun or partial shade
Great for Edges and the middle of a border
Bees & Butterflies Bees
For Cutting Yes
Care Cut back after the first flush to get more flowers. Cats like to roll in them, especially if they are at the front of a border

× *faassenii* A neat, bushy, mounding plant with soft-grey leaves, this variety has short, leafy spikes of tiny, pale-lavender flowers. May to September. **H × S** 45cm × 45cm. AGM

× *faassenii* 'Kit Cat' Shorter, more compact than the previous plant, it has soft-blue flowers and grey leaves. May to September. **H × S** 30cm × 30cm

govaniana This graceful, late-flowering, plant bears long, pale-yellow flowers at well-spaced intervals up slender, branched stems. The leaves are soft green. Will not thrive in soils that are cold and wet over winter. August to September. **H × S** 90cm × 45cm

***grandiflora* 'Dawn to Dusk'** Only a few nepetas have pink flowers. This variety produces dense spikes of pale-pink flowers that sit in mauve calyces. June to September. **H × S** 90cm × 75cm

***grandiflora* 'Wild Cat'** Free-flowering and upright, this bushy nepeta produces attractive heads of soft violet-blue flowers. June to September. **H × S** 90cm × 75cm

Morina longifolia

Nepeta × faassenii

Nepeta × faassenii 'Kit Cat'

Nepeta govaniana

Nepeta grandiflora 'Dawn to Dusk'

Nepeta grandiflora 'Wild Cat'

***racemosa* 'Snowflake'** A low, spreading plant with soft grey-green leaves and spikes of tiny, blue-tinted, white flowers. May to September. **H × S** 45cm × 45cm

***racemosa* 'Walker's Low'** The spikes of violet-blue flowers form a neat mound with grey leaves. May to September. **H × S** 60cm × 60cm. AGM

sibirica A very upright, open and airy plant with big, loose spikes of large, violet-blue flowers. These are carried on thick stems with big, mid-green leaves. June to September. **H × S** 80cm × 60cm

'Six Hills Giant' This excellent, floriferous plant creates a big, blue mound of long stems with small, mid-green leaves that terminate in whorls of little, true-blue flowers. Lovely in drifts among other plants or at the front of a large border. June to September. **H × S** 120cm × 90cm

Nepeta racemosa 'Snowflake'

Nepeta racemosa 'Walker's Low'

Nepeta sibirica

Nepeta 'Six Hills Giant' with *Gillenia trifoliata* and *Veronicastrum virginicum* 'Fascination'

OENOTHERA (Evening primrose)

Masses of flower buds on leafy stems open into large, cup-shaped blooms, each lasting for just a day. Oil is extracted from the seeds.

Needs Well-drained soil in sun
Great for Front of the border
Bees & Butterflies Yes
For Cutting No
Care Trouble free

macrocarpa A prostrate plant with long stems of large, cupped, canary-yellow flowers and long, mid-green leaves. July to September. **H × S** 23cm × 60cm. AGM

'Summer Sun' An upright plant, that tends to tumble forward. Clusters of saucer-shaped, yellow flowers open from red buds on red-tinged stems with deep-green leaves. July to August. **H × S** 60cm × 60cm

OMPHALODES (Navelwort)

verna Early to bloom with pretty sprays of soft-blue flowers held just above a slowly spreading mound of heart-shaped leaves. March to May. **H × S** 25cm × 45cm

Needs Well-drained soil in shade or partial shade
Great for Front of the border
Bees & Butterflies No
For Cutting No
Care Trouble free

OPHIOPOGON (Mondo grass)

planiscapus **'Nigrescens'** Black foliage is unusual in plants. This spreading perennial has grassy tufts of long, matt-black, evergreen leaves and short stems topped with tight spikes of small, lilac-pink flowers. July to August. **H × S** 23cm × 45cm. AGM

Needs Well-drained soil in sun or partial shade
Great for Front of the border and pots
Bees & Butterflies No
For Cutting No
Care Can be slow to establish

ORIGANUM (Marjoram)

laevigatum **'Herrenhausen'** This gently creeping, bushy plant is a magnet for bees and butterflies. The tiny, mauve-pink flowers are borne in small, tight clusters up slender, dark red stems with rounded, dark green, mildly aromatic leaves. July to September. **H × S** 45cm × 60cm. AGM

Needs Well-drained soil in sun
Great for Front of the border
Bees & Butterflies Yes
For Cutting Yes
Care Trouble free

Oenothera macocarpa

Oenothera 'Summer Sun'

Omphalodes verna

Ophiopogon planiscapus 'Nigrescens'

Origanum laevigatum 'Herrenhausen'

Paeonia

(Peony) The large, often blousy flowers of peonies are among the most beautiful of all perennials and have been grown in gardens for centuries. Originating in China, peonies were cultivated in medieval Europe by Benedictine monks, who used the seeds and roots medicinally. Today peonies are classic border plants, but although dramatic, the flowering period can be short. To compensate, they produce a handsome clump of deeply divided foliage that is attractive from the moment the succulent shoots appear in spring until the autumn-tinted leaves die down. Once established, peonies are easy to grow, need little attention, and are the longest-lived of all perennials. The date of introduction, given in the descriptions after the variety and the name of breeder, is testament to their longevity.

HERBACEOUS PEONIES

In this book all the peonies are herbaceous. These are unlike woody tree peonies – which are usually listed as shrubs – in that the top growth dies right back in autumn. New shoots begin to break through the ground as early as February when the days start to lengthen. By mid-May (in our part of the country) the buds have filled out and, depending on the variety, they open from late May until late June.

INTERSECTIONAL PEONIES

A quiet revolution has been occurring in the peony world. The first crosses between tree and herbaceous peonies, were made in the 1960s but the resulting plants weren't available to gardeners until the 1990s. These fabulous plants, known as intersectional peonies, include the best of both types. The flowers, which can be up to 25cm across, are carried on short woody stems above handsome, leathery, deeply cut leaves that often take on lovely autumn colour before cleanly dropping off. Despite having woody stems these are herbaceous. The plant increases outwards, rather than upwards, and has a neat, broad, bushy habit. New shoots emerge from the bottom of each woody stem. Intersectional peonies are easy to grow and establish, and flower at the same time as other herbaceous peonies.

FLOWER SHAPE

Peony flowers come in four shapes. The following terms are used in the descriptions:

- **Single** Flowers have a single or double row of petals
- **Japanese** These have outer 'guard' petals and a centre of staminodes (*see* box)
- **Semi-double** Flowers have three or more rows of petals
- **Double** These have lots of petals and form a 'powder-puff' or domed crown

Paeonia 'Madame Calot' and *P.* 'Barbara' blooming in our peony field, June

Single-flowered peony 'Athena'

Semi-double flowered peony 'Liebchen'

Japanese-type peony 'Largo'

Double peony 'Better Times'

PEONY TERMS USED

CARPELS The centre 'pod' where the seeds are produced

GUARD PETALS The outer petals

PETALOIDS These look like slender petals, but are sepals or bracts

STAMINODES Resembling very thin, central petals, these sterile stamens are usually a feature of Japanese peony flowers

FLOWERING PERIOD

As with all perennials, flowering depends on where you live in the country. At our nursery, located in the middle of the UK, peonies tend to flower from the last week of May to the third week of June, with each variety blooming very early, early, mid-season, or late within this period.

PEONIES FOR CUTTING

Most peonies make good cut flowers. I recommend these particular varieties, which last for a long time (up to 10 days) in water.

'Barbara'	'Kansas'
'Bowl of Beauty'	'Myrtle Gentry'
'Bridal Icing'	'Nancy Nora'
'Catharina Fontijn'	'Pink Dawn'
'Coral Charm'	'Sarah Bernhardt'
'Duchesse de Nemours'	'Shirley Temple'

SCENT

Many peonies are fragrant. In some varieties the scent is light; in others it is released only after the flowers have been picked and placed in a vase. Scent depends on the time of day, where in the garden the plant is grown (a warm spot for instance) and, of course, your nose! Some good scented varieties are listed below, but there are many others. Information about fragrance is given in each plant's description.

'Alexander Fleming'	'Krinkled White'
'Baroness Schroeder'	'Laura Dessert'
'Bouquet Perfect'	'Monsieur Jules Elie'
'Bridal Icing'	'My Pal Rudy'
'Catharina Fontijn'	'Myrtle Gentry'
'Claire de Lune'	'Nancy Nora'
'Edulis Superba'	'Pillow Talk'
'Festiva Maxima'	'Raspberry Sundae'
'Helen Hayes'	'Tom Eckhardt'
'Honey Gold'	

GROWING PEONIES

Peonies need a soil that does not become waterlogged at any time during the year. A good, well-drained loam is ideal, but they are just as happy in a clay soil provided it does not stay wet. These are plants of open grassland so prefer full sun, although they will tolerate a light, shady spot.

Peonies can take up to three years to flower, but once established can live for more than 50 years. As with roses, try not to plant peonies where other peonies have been grown in the past.

Planting time

A peony's roots grow once the leaves have died-back in autumn, so the best time to plant is between October and March. Although some advise against putting peonies in the ground after December, I've had no problem planting them in spring.

Dividing

Contrary to received wisdom, peonies really do not mind being moved, especially if they are not divided. However, if a plant has become too large and needs to be divided, make sure the transplanted clumps have at least three 'eyes' (leaf buds).

Planting distances

After five years, each peony plant will have grown to take up approximately one square metre, so they should be planted about 75cm to 90cm apart.

The leaves of intersectional peonies are thick, leathery, and disease-free. In autumn they drop off neatly and cleanly

Planting

It is important to plant herbaceous peonies with the eyes no more than 2cm below the soil. If they are buried any deeper, they may not flower.

Maintaining

If you want to feed peonies put only a ring of very well-rotted manure around the dormant plant in winter. Be sure not to cover the plant as the 'eyes' may rot as they grow.

Top growth can be removed when it dies back. If you have intersectional peonies, you can cut the woody stems back to the ground to tidy up the plant. This is optional, but it won't harm the plant.

PROBLEMS AND SOLUTIONS

The most common ailment peonies suffer from is botrytis, a fungal disease that is more prevalent during warm, damp weather. Evidence of it can be found at the base of the stem or on the buds, which become brown and mouldy. Remove infected foliage and spray the plant with a fungicide.

Failure to flower

I am frequently asked why a peony has not flowered and there are usually three main reasons:

- The peony has been planted too deeply. Lift the plant in autumn and replant at the correct depth.
- If the plant has become too dry during the spring growing season, the buds will fail to swell and look dried up.
- The plant is growing in a very shady spot, which can lead to dry roots.

Leaves

Brown spots may appear on leaves later in the summer, usually in August, just before the plant starts to enter the dormant state. There is no need to worry about them.

Ants

I have been asked how to get rid of ants on peony flower buds. The answer is: don't. In my experience, ants do no harm. Appearing as the bud swells, they feed on the sugary substance it exudes, and may even help the bud to open properly. As soon as the buds start to open, the ants disappear.

Peony shoots are known as 'eyes'

Red shoots of *Paeonia* 'Shirley Temple' emerging in April

Paeonia 'Shirley Temple', fully grown in May

'Adolphe Rousseau' (Dessert/Mechin 1890) Easy to grow, this peony has double, deep cerise-red flowers. Revealing yellow stamens as they open fully, the blooms are carried on strong, upright stems with dark green foliage. Mid. **H** 90cm

'Alexander Fleming' (Blonk, before 1950) The sweetly scented, double, rich-pink flowers are touched at the edges with silver. When open, the shallow-domed flowers have a loose, swirling centre of petals. Early to mid. **H** 87cm

'Angel Cheeks' (Klehm 1975) The large, ruffled, double, pale-pink flowers are infused with cream and pale to blush-pink as they age. They are mildly fragrant and borne on sturdy stems. Mid. **H** 85cm

'Auguste Dessert' (Dessert 1920) A scented, semi-double, this variety has deep rose-pink flowers with petals that fade to silver-pink around the edges. The flowers open flat revealing a small ring of deep yellow stamens. Good autumn foliage. Mid. **H** 90cm

'Barbara' (Poland before 1986) Great for cutting but not scented. The deep-pink flowers form a tight ball that is surrounded by large guard petals. It has grey leaves and very strong stems. Mid. **H** 90cm

'Baroness Schroeder' (Kelway 1888) The white blooms are not big, but frilly, heavily scented, and domed. Lots of yellow petaloids deep within the centre give the flower an inner glow. Mid to late. **H** 86cm

'Bartzella' (Anderson 1986) An excellent intersectional peony with large, lemon-scented, soft-yellow flowers. The petals form a perfect, frilly rosette around delicate, yellow stamens, which have magenta flares at the base. Mid. **H** 90cm

Paeonia 'Aldophe Rousseau'

Paeonia 'Alexander Fleming'

Paeonia 'Angel Cheeks'

Paeonia 'Auguste Dessert'

Paeonia 'Barbara'

Paeonia 'Baroness Schroeder'

Paeonia 'Bartzella'

Paeonia 'Bouquet Perfect'

Paeonia 'Bowl of Cream'

Paeonia 'Buckeye Belle'

'Bouquet Perfect' (Tischler 1987) This lovely, rose-scented peony has perfectly shaped, bright-pink flowers. A swirling ball of petals is circled by a saucer of large guard petals. As it ages, the centre pales in colour around the edges. Mid to late. **H** 90cm

'Bowl of Beauty' (Hoogendoorn 1949) This deservedly popular variety is also free flowering. Its bright-pink guard petals encircle a ball of pale-lemon, ribbon-like staminodes. Mid. **H** 90cm

'Bowl of Cream' (Klehm 1963) Each smooth, creamy-white petal curves inwards, forming a bowl-like centre. The flowers are double and scented; the leaves are large and grey-green. Early. **H** 78cm

'Bridal Icing' (Klehm 1959) At the centre of the scented, open flower, a ball of slender, cream and white petals looks rather like a scoop of ice cream. As the flower ages, the white petals extend out into a pompom. The flower stems are strong. Mid. **H** 75cm

'Buckeye Belle' (Mains 1956) This early-blooming plant has fabulous, cupped flowers with velvety, deep-red petals. These are tinged with brown and purple and open around a ring of stamens. Early. **H** 75cm

'Catharina Fontijn' (Van der Valk/Van der Zwet 1952) As the heavily scented flower opens up from a soft-pink dome, it evolves into a white rosette and reveals a ring of stamens. Mid. **H** 90cm

'Claire de Lune' (White-Wild & Son 1954) An absolutely beautiful plant. The single, sweetly scented, pale-lemon flowers have a central boss of delicate, yellow stamens. It has red stems and large, deep-green leaves. Very early. **H** 90cm

Paeonia 'Bowl of Beauty'

Paeonia 'Bridal Icing'

Paeonia 'Catharina Fontijn'

Paeonia 'Claire de Lune'

'Cora Louise' (Anderson 1986) An intersectional peony, this bears glistening, white, semi-double flowers with yellow stamens. At the base of each petal is a striking magenta flare. Mid. **H** 75cm

'Coral Charm' (Wissing 1964) Impressive for the size of the semi-double, scented, coral flowers alone. They open into deep goblets with loose, golden stamens, the flower colour softening to orange. The long, red stems need staking but the flowers are excellent for cutting, lasting ten days or longer. The leaves are large, deep-green, and shiny. Early to mid. **H** 90cm or more

'Cytherea' (Saunders 1953) The semi-double, bright rose-pink flowers have three or four rows of petals. Goblet-shaped when first open, the blooms age to form a relaxed cup. The flowers are held on short, strong stems with mid-green leaves. Early. **H** 75cm

'Dinner Plate' (Klehm 1968) Aptly named, the large soft-pink flowers open into flat rosettes, their soft, silky petals paler along the edges. Although they are carried on strong, thick stems with thick, leathery, dark green leaves, the flower heads may need staking. Late. **H** 110cm.

'Doreen' (Sass 1949) This Japanese peony has bright-pink guard petals that fade to paler pink as the flower opens. They are ranged round a pompom-like centre of frilly, ribbon-like, cream staminodes. It blooms over a long period. Mid. **H** 81cm

'Duchesse de Nemours' (Calot 1856) The double, white flowers of this old yet reliable variety are beautifully scented and excellent for cutting. The loose petals are tinted yellow at the base. Mid. **H** 90cm

Paeonia 'Coral Charm'

Paeonia 'Cora Louise'

Paeonia 'Cytherea'

Paeonia 'Dinner Plate'

Paeonia 'Doreen'

Paeonia 'Duchesse de Nemours'

Paeonia 'Edulis Superba'

Paeonia 'Eliza Lundy'

Paeonia 'Elsa Sass'

Paeonia 'First Arrival'

Paeonia 'Festiva Maxima'

Paeonia 'Garden Treasure'

'Edulis Superba' (Lemon 1824) Among the oldest surviving varieties still grown, this has heavily scented, deep rose-pink blooms that form shallow domes. Despite having rather weak stems, the flowers are great for cutting. Early to mid. **H** 85cm

'Eliza Lundy' (Krekler 1975) A low-growing plant with short stems, it produces small, rich-red, double flowers with ruffled petals held in a ball by larger, outer guard petals. The glossy, mid-green leaves create a generally upright mound that may flop over at the edges. Early to mid. **H** 71cm

'Elsa Sass' (Sass 1930) Initially shaped like a goblet, the large, white flowers open into a shallow bowl. The thick, satiny, interlaced petals give off a creamy glow at the base. The leaves are dark green. Late. **H** 71cm

'Festiva Maxima' (Miellez 1851) Loosely formed and scented, the double, white flowers display a few red streaks and have large guard petals. A free-flowering variety that is good for cutting. Mid. **H** 90cm

'First Arrival' (Anderson 1986) A delightful intersectional peony with large, semi-double, glossy, lavender-pink flowers that soften to pink with age. Each bloom opens at even intervals across an open, spreading bush with deeply divided leaves that turn red in autumn. Early. **H** 80cm

'Garden Treasure' (Hollingsworth 1984) My first intersectional peony, this superb plant was given to me by the breeder. The large, semi-double, primrose-yellow flowers are fragrant, their petals forming a ruff around a ring of golden stamens and distinctive, green carpels. Large, mid-green, divided leaves create a handsome rounded, broad mound. Mid. **H** 90cm

'Gay Paree' (Auten 1933) The dainty flowers have rich rose-pink guard petals and a large centre of ribbon-like, cream staminodes that are stained pink along the edges. The flowers are held upright. Mid. **H** 90cm

'Goldilocks' (Gilbertson 1975) The nicely scented, ball-shaped, soft-yellow flower has intertwined petals and large guard petals. It might take a few years to produce the most glamorous blooms. Mid. **H** 75cm

'Helen Hayes' (Murawska 1943) Carried on strong stems with dark green, glossy leaves the scented, double, deep-pink flowers have notched petal edges. The head forms a high dome with the shorter inner petals creating a central bowl. Mid. **H** 90cm

'Henry Bockstoce' (Bockstoce 1955) Resembling an old rose, the big, double, scarlet-red flowers have tightly woven, thick, shiny petals. The long, thick stems might need staking, but they make the blooms great for cutting. Mid **H** 105cm

'Hillary' (Anderson 1999) This may not be the most shapely of intersectional peonies, but it carries a great profusion of shaggy, semi-double, raspberry red-stained, cream flowers. Mid to late. **H** 90cm

'Honey Gold' (Klehm before 1966) Pure-white guard petals encase long, fringed, yellow staminodes on this long-flowering and very fragrant variety. These fill out to form a dome, sometimes with extra flutes of petals in the centre. Early. **H** 76cm

'Inspecteur Lavergne' (Doriat 1924) A classic peony with long stems of ball-shaped, double, rich-red flowers that have silver-lined, frilly edged petals. Mid. **H** 90cm

Paeonia 'Gay Paree'

Paeonia 'Goldilocks'

Paeonia 'Helen Hayes'

Paeonia 'Henry Bockstoce'

Paeonia 'Hillary'

Paeonia 'Honey Gold'

Paeonia 'Inspecteur Lavergne'

'Jan van Leeuwen' (Van Leeuwen 1928) One of the most perfect white peonies. The cupped, pristine flowers are filled with golden staminodes and carried on evenly sized, upright stems to form a neat mound. Mid. **H** 90cm

'Julia Rose' (Anderson 1991) A stunning plant with large, silky, semi-double blooms. These start out red then quickly fade to a rose-pink, warmed by gold tones at the base of the petals. The thick, long, deeply divided foliage is burnished with pewter in autumn. Mid. **H** 80cm

'Kansas' (Bigger 1940) The compact, frilly flowers are large doubles and the colour is a clear yet rich shade between pink and red. They sit above a robust clump of leaves on upright stems, which makes this a good variety for cutting. Early to mid. **H** 90cm

'Krinkled White' (Brand 1928) Resembling crêpe paper, the petals of this heavily scented, single, pure-white flower surround a boss of yellow stamens. The straight stems rise above shiny, light green leaves. Early. **H** 81cm

'Lancaster Imp' (Klehm 1987) Short and upright, this plant has delightful double, pure-white flowers. The slender petals entwine to form a raised ball that sits on enlarged guard petals. Early. **H** 60cm

'Laura Dessert' (Dessert 1913) A scented variety with white guard petals that form a saucer for the ball of slim, fringed, cream petaloids. As the flowers age the petaloids turn white. Mid. **H** 90cm

Paeonia 'Julia Rose'

Paeonia 'Jan van Leeuwen'

Paeonia 'Kansas'

Paeonia 'Krinkled White'

Paeonia 'Lancaster Imp'

Paeonia 'Laura Dessert'

'Mai Fleuri' (Lemoine 1905) The deeply cupped, single, soft-pink flowers have translucent petals and a centre of fine, yellow stamens. They may not flower for long, but the large, bright-green leaves are very handsome. Early. **H** 75cm

'May Apple' (Wolf 1977) Single, mid-pink flowers have a thick boss of golden stamens. Forming a deep cup, the shiny petals fade to white at the base. The foliage is bright green. Early to mid. **H** 90cm

mlokosewitschii I find this fleeting beauty difficult to grow, as it needs warm, well-drained soil. The soft-lemon, cupped flowers are carried on upright stems above large, glaucous leaves. Very early. **H** 85cm

'Madame Calot' (Miellez 1856) Scented, small, double flowers flushed with soft pink take on tones of pale yellow and blush-pink when the petals emerge. The flower fades to near white. Early. **H** 90cm

'Monsieur Jules Elie' (Crousse 1888) Strongly rose-scented, the large, double, rose-pink flowers open into a high dome. The petals curve inwards and are edged with silver. Mid. **H** 90cm

'Moon of Nippon' (Auten 1936) Very free-flowering and quintessentially Japanese, this peony has large, white blooms carried on stiff stems. The small, yellow centres swell as the flowers age. Mid. **H** 90cm

'Mr G. F. Hemerik' (Van Leeuwen 1930) Deep-pink petals, fading slightly with age, surround a perfect dome of broad, cream staminodes. This Japanese peony has distinctive, crinkled leaves. Mid. **H** 90cm

Paeonia 'Mai Fleuri'

Paeonia 'May Apple'

Paeonia mlokosewitschii

Paeonia 'Madame Calot'

Paeonia 'Monsieur Jules Elie'

Paeonia 'Moon of Nippon'

Paeonia 'Mr G. F. Hemerik'

Paeonia 'My Pal Rudy'

Paeonia 'Myrtle Gentry'

Paeonia 'Nancy Nora'

Paeonia 'Nice Gal'

Paeonia 'Nippon Beauty'

Paeonia 'Nosegay'

Paeonia 'Nymphe'

'My Pal Rudy' (Klehm 1953) Perfect for small gardens, this has double, scented, pale-pink flowers with notched petals that open into a flat rosette to reveal a small ring of yellow stamens. The leaves are deep green and glossy. Late. **H** 81cm

'Myrtle Gentry' (Brand 1925) Very beautiful, like a perfect old rose, the large, double, scented, blush-pink flowers fade to white with age. They are carried on stiff stems above matt, mid-green leaves. Excellent for cutting. Mid. **H** 90cm

'Nancy Nora' (Bernstein 1942) The large, scented, pale blush-pink flowers have equal-sized petals and a dipped centre, rather like a lovely old rose. Upright stems with soft-green leaves make this variety good for cutting. Mid. **H** 90cm

'Nice Gal' (Krekler 1965) This neat plant has semi-double, deep-pink flowers. They open into a broad rosette, showing off the small, yellow stamens. Mid. **H** 75cm

'Nippon Beauty' (Auten 1927) The deepest, dark red of this Japanese peony's blooms is like the colour of a garnet. The same shade is displayed in the central boss of yellow-lined staminodes. Late. **H** 90cm

'Nosegay' (Saunders 1950) Although not very long-lasting, the single, delicate shell-pink flowers with petals like silk, are beautiful. They are carried above deeply divided, mid-green leaves. Early. **H** 65cm

'Nymphe' (Dessert 1913) A free-flowering plant with upward-facing, strongly scented, single blooms in deep pink. Upright stems rise above a neat mound of dark green leaves. This always sets seed. Late. **H** 90cm

officinalis **'Anemoniflora Rosea'** This Japanese peony is an absolute delight when mature. The shallowly domed, bright pink flowers are carried on stiff stems with grey-green leaves. Early. **H** 75cm

officinalis **'Rubra Plena'** A traditional double, red cottage-garden peony. The ball-shaped, scented, deepest-crimson flowers have frilly petals that form small rosettes. The blooms are carried on long, rather lax stems above lush, deep-green leaves. Early. **H** 75cm

'Paul M. Wild' (Wild 1964) Definitely one of the best reds we have grown, this variety has luxurious, double, richest-red flowers with velvety petals that form a neat dome. The leaves are bright green. Mid. **H** 90cm

'Picotee' (Saunders 1949) A lovely, rather brief-flowering variety with single, white flowers tinted a soft pink that darkens to magenta at the petal edges. Ruffled leaves form an attractive mound. Early. **H** 60cm

'Pillow Talk' (Klehm 1973) Like perfect powder-puffs, the clear-pink, scented flowers are freely produced on strong stems above dark green leaves. Mid. **H** 90cm

'Pink Dawn' (Sass 1946) Easy to grow, this peony also produces lots of blooms that appear pink. Look closer and you will see the petals are white but covered with deep-pink dots. Stiff, upright stems make this a good cut flower. Mid. **H** 90cm

'Pink Parfait' (Klehm 1975) At first dome-shaped, the scented flowers with deep, rather shaggy, rose-pink petals open into a flatter crown. The large, satiny leaves are deep green. Late. **H** 83cm

Paeonia officinalis 'Anemoniflora Rosea'

Paeonia officinalis 'Rubra Plena'

Paeonia 'Paul M. Wild'

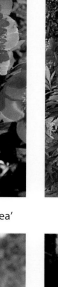

Paeonia 'Picotee'

Paeonia 'Pillow Talk'

Paeonia 'Pink Dawn'

Paeonia 'Pink Parfait'

Paeonia 'Raspberry Sundae'

Paeonia 'Red Charm'

'Raspberry Sundae' (Klehm 1968) Large and high-domed, these fragrant flowers consist of rings of cream petaloids and soft pink-flushed, white petals. The flower grows into a true ice-cream sundae on long, rather relaxed stems. Mid. **H** 90cm

'Red Charm' (Glasscock 1944) This excellent plant has double, glossy-red flowers that are long-lasting. Held on stiff stems, the blooms form a domed ball of serrated petals within large guard petals. Early. **H** 81cm

'Red Red Rose' (Saunders 1952) Eye-catching is the word for this plant. The large, semi-double, bright-scarlet flowers have long, yellow stamens. They are carried on thick, straight stems above large, mid-green leaves. Early. **H** 90cm

'Roselette' (Saunders 1950) One of the first peonies to flower, this has beautiful, single, soft-pink flowers with large, golden stamens. Very early. **H** 90cm

'Sarah Bernhardt' (Lemoine 1906) The scented, double, pure-pink flowers of this classic variety are tinted with silver around the edges. Long stems make the flowers excellent for cutting. Late. **H** 90cm

'Scarlet O'Hara' (Falk-Glasscock 1956) Each lightly scented flower, which looks like a big, scarlet poppy, lasts for up to ten days. As the flowers age, the petals get bigger and fade to deep pink. Early. **H** 90cm

'Serene Pastel' (Klehm 2000) This short plant carries its white blooms, with tints of salmon-pink, on strong stems. The flowers open into a flatter rosette shape, revealing a ring of stamens. Early. **H** 80cm

Paeonia 'Red Red Rose'

Paeonia 'Roselette'

Paeonia 'Sarah Bernhardt'

Paeonia 'Scarlet O'Hara'

Paeonia 'Serene Pastel'

'Shirley Temple' (Smirnow before 1948) A free-flowering plant with big, glamorous balls of double, white flowers with pink-tinged guard petals. Long flower stems make this an excellent flower for cutting. Mid. **H** 86cm

'Sorbet' This lovely plant was found growing in a South Korean orchard in 1986 by a Dutch perennial specialist. Large and spectacular, the soft-pink petals of the flower are interlaced with pink-tinged, lemon petaloids. Mid. **H** 90cm

'Sword Dance' (Auten 1933) A stunning Japanese peony with a ruff of silky, bright-red guard petals surrounding a large, loose dome of red-tinged, yellow staminodes. Late. **H** 87cm

'Tom Eckhardt' (Krekler 1965) The scented flowers have fuchsia-pink guard petals and a large dome of cream staminodes and may produce a few more pink inner petals. The whole flower pales with age and sits above very large, bright-green leaves. Late. **H** 90cm

'Top Brass' (Klehm 1968) A sophisticated flower with white guard petals, a distinctive domed centre made from of rings of creamy petals, and a central flute of very pale-pink petals. An upright plant. Mid. **H** 85cm

wittmanniana (Klehm 1968) I grow the pink form of this usually white-flowered peony in the semi-shade of trees. The petals are almost translucent with undertones of yellow and the big, shiny, green leaves form a neat mound. Early. **H** 85cm

'Zuzu' (Krekler 1955) Delightful and scented, the semi-double flowers open a delicate blush-pink and fade to pure white. They are carried on short, stiff stems. Mid. **H** 75cm

Paeonia 'Shirley Temple'

Paeonia 'Sorbet'

Paeonia 'Sword Dance'

Paeonia 'Tom Eckhardt'

Paeonia 'Top Brass'

Paeonia wittmanniana (pink form)

Paeonia 'Zuzu'

Papaver orientale 'Black and White'

Papaver orientale 'Burning Heart'

PAPAVER (Oriental poppy)

Among the most opulent of perennial flowers, the very large, often cupped blooms of poppies really draw the eye into a border. At the centre of the papery petals, the distinctive, knob-shaped seed pod turns fluffy with stamens. The tall, hairy stems rise above a thick clump of long, rough, mid-green leaves.

Needs Well-drained soil in sun
Great for Middle of the border
Bees & Butterflies Bees
For Cutting Yes, but the stems have a milky sap so need to be sealed in hot water
Care Foliage dies back after flowering, re-emerging from late summer onwards, so think about what to plant near them as a temporary measure to cover up the gap. I use later-flowering asters such as *Aster* 'Little Carlow'. Poppy roots can be difficult to eradicate. When you lift the plant, any pieces left in the ground will re-grow. Some oriental poppy varieties need staking

orientale **'Black and White'** Stunning when at its best, this rather lax variety has large, semi-double, pure-white petals. These display narrow, black flares at the base. May to June. **H × S** 80cm × 70cm. AGM

orientale **'Burning Heart'** A fairly new variety with perfectly shaped, semi-double, deep reddish-pink flowers. This needs no staking. May to June. **H × S** 75cm × 70cm

orientale **'Forncett Summer'** The big, exotic, salmon-pink flowers are brushed with maroon and the edges of the petals are fringed. It is an extremely free-flowering variety, but may need staking. May to June. **H × S** 75cm × 70cm

Papaver orientale 'Forncett Summer'

Papaver orientale Goliath Group 'Beauty of Livermere'

Papaver orientale 'Karine'

Papaver orientale 'Mrs Perry'

***orientale* Goliath Group 'Beauty of Livermere'** Held at the top of stiff stems are big, silky, vibrant, rich-red blooms with black spots at each petal's base. May not come true if grown from seed. May to June. **H × S** 105cm × 80cm. AGM

***orientale* 'Karine'** Petite and more delicate than other oriental poppies, this bears shallow-cupped, soft salmon-pink flowers with maroon basal flares. These are carried on short, but stiff stems. May to June. **H × S** 75cm × 70cm. AGM

***orientale* 'Mrs Perry'** An old, but reliable variety with delicate, deeply cupped, soft salmon-pink flowers with black 'thumb prints' at the base of each petal. May need staking. May to June. **H × S** 90cm × 80cm

***orientale* 'Patty's Plum'** During the 1990s this was THE poppy to grow owing to its glamorous, ruffled, deep plum-mauve flowers. The tall stems might need some staking. May to June. **H × S** 90cm × 80cm

***orientale* 'Perry's White'** A classic variety with pure-white flowers marked at the base with black blotches. The marking may stain the bottom of the petals dark maroon. Stems may need staking. May to June. **H × S** 90cm × 80cm

***orientale* 'Picotée'** The ruffled flowers of this poppy display two distinct colours. Its white petals are heavily and unevenly stained from the edges down with orange-red. Definitely needs staking. May to June. **H × S** 80cm × 70cm

***orientale* 'Türkenlouis'** With its large, vibrant-red flowers fringed along the edges, this is beautiful and eye-catching. May need support. May to June. **H × S** 90cm × 80cm

Papaver orientale 'Patty's Plum'

Papaver orientale 'Perry's White'

Papaver orientale 'Picotée'

Papaver orientale 'Türkenlouis'

Penstemon 'Alice Hindley'

Penstemon 'Andenken an Friedrich Hahn'

PENSTEMON

These free-flowering, bushy plants have woody stems that drip with colourful foxglove-like flowers. I find them difficult to blend into a border, especially in a cottage garden-style planting, but for those with more formal borders, they are perfect, and need no staking, They do well in containers.

Needs Well-drained soil in sun
Great for Middle of the border; containers
Bees & Butterflies Bees
For Cutting Yes
Care Can be tender in cold areas of the country and may not thrive in soil that remains wet over winter. Prune the woody stems to a leaf joint in spring

'Alice Hindley' Large, soft-lilac flowers with white throats rise above a rather loose clump of shiny, mid-green leaves. July to September. **H × S** 90cm × 45cm. AGM

'Andenken an Friedrich Hahn' This handsome plant is covered with long, slim, bright-crimson trumpets. It forms an open, upright bush with red stems and slender, mid-green leaves. July to September. **H × S** 80cm × 50cm. AGM

digitalis **'Husker Red'** I would grow this plant for the deep-red leaves alone, although the spikes of slender, white, lilac-tinged trumpets do round things off nicely. July to September. **H × S** 75cm × 60cm

'Raven' Beautifully coloured, the large, rich-purple flowers look particularly dark and lustrous in certain lights. The leaves are mid-green. July to September. **H × S** 90cm × 45cm. AGM

Penstemon digitalis 'Husker Red'

Penstemon 'Raven'

Penstemon 'Rich Ruby'

Penstemon 'Stapleford Gem'

Penstemon 'White Bedder'

'Rich Ruby' The broad, deep-burgundy flowers, purple around the lips and striped white inside, are carried in short spikes above a clump of slender, glossy, mid-green leaves. July to September. **H × S** 90cm × 75cm. AGM

'Stapleford Gem' An attractive, statuesque plant with glowing, lilac flowers, tinged with blue. These stand out in horizontal layers all the way up the stems. This variety is often confused with 'Sour Grapes'. July to September. **H × S** 90cm × 60cm. AGM

'White Bedder' A neat plant with slim, pure-white trumpets that become tinged with pink. It is also sold under various other names, including 'Snowstorm'. July to September. **H × S** 70cm × 60cm. AGM

PERSICARIA (Bistort)

Although bistorts may not be the most 'flowery' of perennials, they are among the longest-blooming. Great quantities of flower spikes packed with tiny stars or bell-shaped flowers are carried with enormous grace, over many months. The stems are slender and rise above a mound or carpet of weed-excluding leaves.

Needs Soil that remains moist in sun or partial shade
Great for All parts of the border
Bees & Butterflies Bees
For Cutting Yes
Care Trouble free and easy to grow in the right soil. *P. amplexicaulis* hybrids will self-seed freely

affinis **'Darjeeling Red'** Long 'pokers' of tiny, soft-pink flowers are carried just above a thick carpet of slim, mid-green leaves. These turn brick-red as they age, creating interesting mixed tones. Other very similar varieties include *P. affinis* 'Superba' and 'Donald Lowndes'. June to September. **H × S** 30cm × 90cm. AGM

amplexicaulis **'Alba'** Thread-thin spikes of white flowers open from bronze buds and rise elegantly from a mound of big, oval leaves. Very effective when planted against a background of dark foliage. July to September. **H × S** 90cm × 90cm

amplexicaulis **'Blackfield'** A plant with rich-red flowers opening from very dark buds, giving the spikes a dark red tinge. The leaves are big, oval, and mid-green. July to September. **H × S** 105cm × 90cm

amplexicaulis **'Fat Domino'** On this very open and upright plant, the long, fat spikes of rich-red flowers make a big impact. It has slender stems and large, mid-green leaves. July to October. **H × S** 90cm × 75cm

Persicaria affinis 'Darjeeling Red'

Persicaria amplexicaulis 'Blackfield'

Persicaria amplexicaulis 'Alba'

Persicaria amplexicaulis 'Fat Domino'

Persicaria amplexicaulis 'Inverleith'

Persicaria amplexicaulis 'Orange Field'

Persicaria amplexicaulis
'Jo and Guido's Form'

Persicaria amplexicaulis 'Rosea'

***amplexicaulis* 'Inverleith'** Stumpy and profuse spikes of tiny, pink-red flowers tumble from a dense mound of mid-green leaves. July to October. **H × S** 60cm × 75cm

***amplexicaulis* 'Jo and Guido's Form'** Slim flower spikes in a pretty shade of bright pink thickly cover a mound of big, dark green leaves. July to September. **H × S** 90cm × 90cm

***amplexicaulis* 'Orange Field'** A handsome plant with upright spikes of coral-pink flowers sitting proudly above a mound of large, oval, mid-green leaves. July to October. **H × S** 90cm × 90cm

***amplexicaulis* 'Rosea'** Slender, soft-pink spikes seem to hang in the air like strings of beads on this gently coloured plant with big, mid-green leaves. July to September. **H × S** 90cm × 90cm

***amplexicaulis* 'Taurus'** A continuous stream of slender, bright-red spikes creates a colourful swathe above large, handsome leaves. *P. amplexicaulis* 'Firetail' is similar. July to September. **H × S** 90 cm × 90cm

***bistorta* 'Superba'** This lush, spreading plant has big, oval, soft-green leaves, rather like those of a wild dock, and short pokers of tiny, baby-pink flowers. It is ideal for damper soils. May to June. **H × S** 90cm × 90cm. AGM

polymorpha Enormous, yet self-supporting, this wonderful, unassuming, bushy plant carries big plumes of tiny, cream flowers that become pink with age. The long, sturdy bronze stems have large, mid-green leaves. July to October. **H × S** 200cm × 150cm

Persicaria amplexicaulis 'Taurus'

Persicaria bistorta 'Superba'

Persicaria polymorpha needs space but is perfect for the back of a border, where it will provide interest well into autumn

Phlomis russeliana

Phlomis tuberosa

Phlox × arendsii 'Hesperis'

PHLOMIS

This excellent, if very small, group of tough perennials has rough, heart-shaped leaves and hooded flowers carried in tiered whorls up rigidly straight stems. Over winter, the long-lasting stems of *P. russeliana* provide wonderful structure.

Needs Well-drained soil in sun or partial shade, including clay soils
Great for Front of the border
Bees & Butterflies Bees
For Cutting Yes
Care Can be slow to establish, otherwise trouble free

russeliana (Jerusalem sage) A plant with presence. It has hooded, soft-yellow flowers carried in thick rings all the way up the stems. Handsome, sage-green leaves sit in pairs just below the flowers and, at the base, form a weed-suppressing, evergreen carpet. June to August. **H × S** 90cm × 90cm. AGM

tuberosa An elegant plant with whorls of soft-mauve blooms set at intervals up dark red stems with rich-green leaves. The variety *P. tuberosa* 'Amazone' is taller, at 150cm. June to August. **H × S** 120cm × 60cm. AGM

PHLOX

Bright-coloured, luxuriant, and very fragrant, phloxes come in shades of pink, white, and purple. The single flowers are flat and held in large, billowing clusters. They are carried on stiff stems that rarely need any staking. Within a few years, plants will grow into a big clump.

Needs Well-drained soil in sun or partial shade
Great for Front or middle of the border
Bees & Butterflies Yes
For Cutting Yes
Care When lifting *P. paniculata* types, ensure you clear all roots to prevent re-growth. In damp summers *P. paniculata* can suffer from leaf spot and sometimes powdery mildew

× *arendsii* **'Hesperis'** One of the last phlox to bloom. Tall heads of small, lilac, heavily scented flowers rise from an open clump. July to September. **H × S** 105cm × 75cm

× *arendsii* **'Luc's Lilac'** The heads of delicate pink, magenta-eyed flowers form shallow domes and an airy clump. July to September. **H × S** 90cm × 60cm. AGM

carolina **'Bill Baker'** A trailing phlox that is ideal for the front of a border. The lavender-pink flowers with tiny, white eyes are held in open clusters on red stems. July to October. **H × S** 30cm × 45cm. AGM

Phlox maculata (Early phlox) *There are only few varieties and all flower before the more dramatically coloured Phlox paniculata. Their slender columns of small, flat flowers and slim, mid-green leaves form elegant clumps.*

maculata 'Alpha' A lovely, strongly scented variety with fine, tall heads of small, rich-pink flowers. July to August. **H × S** 90cm × 75cm. AGM

maculata 'Omega' White flowers with small, pale pink-ringed eyes stand tall on neat, upright clumps. July to August. **H × S** 90cm × 75cm. AGM

Phlox paniculata (Border phlox) *Often richly coloured, the individual flowers are quite large, their clusters forming towering or shallow domes. The flowers continue to open over a long period and are carried on stiff stems with, usually, mid-green leaves. There are many, many varieties in this very popular group. In our garden, they look their best during August.*

paniculata 'Amethyst' The domed heads consist of wavy-edged, rosy-lilac coloured flowers. Also sold as 'Lilac Time'. July to September. **H × S** 90cm × 75cm

paniculata 'Blue Paradise' A plant with single, vivid lilac-blue flowers carried in neatly domed clusters on dark purple stems. July to September. **H × S** 90cm × 75cm

paniculata 'Border Gem' A bright coloured plant with tidy clusters of vivid rose-purple flowers that open not only at the tops but also further down the stems. July to September. **H × S** 90cm × 75cm

Phlox × arendsii 'Luc's Lilac'

Phlox carolina 'Bill Baker'

Phlox maculata 'Alpha'

Phlox maculata 'Omega'

Phlox paniculata 'Amethyst'

Phlox paniculata 'Blue Paradise'

Phlox paniculata 'Border Gem'

Phlox paniculata 'Bright Eyes'

Phlox paniculata 'David'

Phlox paniculata 'Discovery'

Phlox paniculata 'Düsterlohe'

Phlox paniculata 'Eva Cullum'

paniculata **'Bright Eyes'** This soft-coloured variety bears domed clusters of pale-pink flowers with bright-pink eyes. July to September. **H × S** 90cm × 75cm

paniculata **'David'** A sturdy and disease-resistant plant with large, tall heads of pure-white flowers. July to September. **H × S** 90cm × 75cm. AGM

paniculata **'Discovery'** More delicate than many *P. paniculata* types, it has shallow heads of soft-pink flowers with magenta eyes. July to September. **H × S** 90cm × 75cm

paniculata **'Düsterlohe'** Sometimes listed as 'Nicky', this variety has round heads of rosy-purple flowers with centres of deep pink. July to August. **H × S** 90cm × 75cm

paniculata **'Eva Cullum'** A heavily scented plant, this bears clusters of bright-pink flowers with darker pink eyes. July to August. **H × S** 90cm × 75cm. AGM

paniculata **'Norah Leigh'** Plants with variegated leaves may not be everyone's cup of tea, but the combination of white-splashed leaves and soft-pink flowers will brighten a dark spot in the garden. July to August. **H × S** 90cm × 75cm. AGM

paniculata **'Prince of Orange'** Although described as orange, the flowers are more orange-pink with small maroon centres. July to August. **H × S** 75cm × 60cm. AGM

paniculata **'Tenor'** The heads of scented, rosy-red flowers are carried on reddish stems with red-tinged, dark green leaves. July to August. **H × S** 80cm × 60cm

paniculata **'Uspekh'** The most strongly scented phlox I have grown, this variety has big, rosy-purple flowers with large, white eyes. Sometimes listed as 'Laura'. July to August. **H × S** 75cm × 60cm. AGM

paniculata **'White Admiral'** A free-flowering plant with towering heads of heavily scented, pure-white flowers that are more star-shaped than round. July to August. **H × S** 90cm × 75cm. AGM

PHUOPSIS

stylosa The short stems of this rather untidy, but useful, ground-covering plant are topped by fluffy, bright-pink flowers like pom-poms. These are carried in profusion above whorls of scented, crisp, light green leaves. May to June. **H × S** 23cm × 60cm

Needs Well-drained soil in sun or partial shade
Great for Front of the border
Bees & Butterflies Bees
For Cutting No
Care Neaten straggly plants by cutting back after flowering; otherwise trouble free

Phlox paniculata 'Prince of Orange'

Phlox paniculata 'Tenor'

Phlox paniculata 'Norah Leigh' with tall
Eupatorium purpureum behind

Phlox paniculata 'Uspekh'

Phlox paniculata 'White Admiral'

Phuopsis stylosa

Physostegia virginiana 'Summer Snow'

Physostegia virginiana var. *speciosa*
'Variegata'

Physostegia virginiana 'Vivid'

Pimpinella major 'Rosea'

Polemonium subsp. *caeruleum* f. *albiflorum*

PHYSOSTEGIA (Obedient plant)

Upright, elegant but not showy, this perennial resembles a short foxglove. Tapering spires of small, tubular flowers – the lips extending outwards – cover a straight stem with long leaves. If you give a flower a gentle push to one side, it will stay put for a while, hence the common name.

Needs Well-drained soil in sun or partial shade
Great for Middle of the border
Bees & Butterflies Bees
For Cutting Yes
Care Trouble free

virginiana var. *speciosa* **'Variegata'** The flowers are a pretty shade of soft mauve, but the attractive cream-edged foliage also looks good on its own. July to September. **H × S** 80cm × 60cm

virginiana **'Summer Snow'** A clean-looking plant carrying stems of purest-white flowers. July to September. **H × S** 80cm × 60cm. AGM

virginiana **'Vivid'** A softly coloured, upright clump, this has pale-mauve flowers. July to September. **H × S** 80cm × 60cm. AGM

PIMPINELLA

major **'Rosea'** (Great burnet saxifrage) Resembling our native cow parsley, but in pink, this bears flat heads of tiny, bright-pink flowers that fade with age. These are carried on branched, upright stems above a loose mound of deeply divided, rich-green leaves. July to August. **H × S** 60cm × 50cm

Needs Soil that remains moist in sun
Great for Front of a border and wild gardens
Bees & Butterflies Bees
For Cutting No
Care Trouble free in the right soil

POLEMONIUM (Jacob's ladder)

Clusters of bell-shaped flowers are ranged all the way up the stems and the attractive divided leaves resemble the rungs of a ladder.

Needs Well-drained soil in sun or partial shade
Great for Front or middle of the border
Bees & Butterflies Bees
For Cutting No
Care Prefers a cooler spot in the garden. Seed-raised varieties are short-lived but may produce seedlings.

subsp. *caeruleum* f. *albiflorum* This white form of *P. caeruleum* (which is usually blue) self-seeds freely. It produces leafy, upright stems topped with sprays of silky, pure-white flowers. June to August. **H × S** 60cm × 45cm

'Lambrook Mauve' A charming, very early flowering variety with sprays of open, soft mauve-pink flowers carried above a broad, relaxed clump of mid-green leaves. May to June. **H × S** 60cm × 75cm

***yezoense* var. *hidakanum* 'Bressingham Purple'** On this upright plant, clusters of violet bells stand out against almost-black stems. The dark green leaves are tinged with red. May to July. **H × S** 60cm × 45cm

POLYGONATUM (Solomon's seal)

× *hybridum* This noble plant prefers shady parts of the garden. Structurally different to many perennials, it has long, arching stems with offset pairs of wing-like, pleated, mid-green leaves. Below them dangle clusters of small, green-rimmed, cream bells. The stems bend gracefully over the ground, forming a canopy. May to June. **H × S** 105cm × 75cm. AGM

Needs Cool, shady spot with moist soil
Great for Woodland or by a north wall
Bees & Butterflies No
For Cutting Yes
Care Trouble free in the right soil

POTENTILLA (Cinquefoil)

Individually, the blooms of this charming, easy-to-grow group may not be dramatic, but they are produced in great quantity. Most varieties have a relaxed shape, the slender, long stems forming a waterfall of colour that makes them useful for edging borders. They resemble strawberries, and have very similar, large leaves.

Needs Well-drained soil in sun or partial shade
Great for Front and middle of the border
Bees & Butterflies Bees
For Cutting No
Care Some potentillas are so lax in habit they will fall forwards. To encourage them to stand taller, plant in the middle of a border among upright plants and the stems will sneak upwards

'Arc-en-ciel' The semi-double, red flowers, highlighted with flecks of yellow, are carried on long, arching stems. June to August. **H × S** 45cm × 45cm

'Esta Ann' A vividly coloured plant. The long, arching stems terminate in sprays of startling bright-yellow flowers with contrasting red flares in the centre. June to August. **H × S** 45cm × 45cm

'Flambeau' A mounding network of long, relaxed, branched stems carries deep-red, semi-double flowers for many weeks. June to August. **H × S** 60cm × 45cm

Polemonium 'Lambrook Mauve'

Polemonium yezoense var. *hidakanum* 'Bressingham Purple'

Polygonatum × *hybridum*

Potentilla 'Arc-en-ciel'

Potentilla 'Esta Ann'

Potentilla 'Flambeau'

'Gibson's Scarlet' Among the most vivid of the red-flowered varieties. Blooms are carried on long, lax stems over many weeks. June to August. **H × S** 45cm × 75cm. AGM

× hopwoodiana A lovely, long-flowering plant with white-edged, soft salmon-pink flowers and long, arching stems. May to August. **H × S** 45cm × 60cm

nepalensis 'Miss Willmott' This seed-raised variety flowers very freely. Its rich-pink, raspberry-centred blooms pale with age. June to August. **H × S** 45cm × 60cm

recta var. sulphurea Upright, well-branched stems are topped with upward-facing, soft primrose-yellow flowers. The jagged, mid-green leaves are carried all the way down the stems. Comes true from seed. June to August. **H × S** 60cm × 45cm

Potentilla × *hopwoodiana*

Potentilla 'Gibson's Scarlet' with *Monarda* 'Cambridge Scarlet' behind

Potentilla nepalensis 'Miss Willmott'

Potentilla recta var. *sulphurea*

Potentilla rupestris

rupestris An early-flowering, rather frothy plant. Pretty, pure-white flowers with yellow centres are held on slender, well-branched stems. May to June. **H × S** 60cm × 75cm

'William Rollison' The eye-catching, semi-double flowers are vermilion at first with flares of yellow. As they age, the blooms turn orange. June to August. **H × S** 60cm × 75cm. AGM

'Yellow Queen' Brilliant-yellow, rosette-shaped flowers are carried on straight stems with soft-green leaves. Richer soils can produce lax growth. June to August. **H × S** 45cm × 45cm

PRIMULA (Primrose)

Of the thousands of primulas available to gardeners, only a limited number are suitable for bigger borders. Fortunately, most are perfect for containers. The primrose family is a charming group of plants with simply shaped flowers, which are often scented, springing from a rosette of long, broad, mid-green leaves.

Needs Soil that remains reliably moist in partial shade or shade
Great for Woodlands, but some are suitable for pond edges and any damp soil
Bees & Butterflies Bees
For Cutting Yes
Care Given the right site and soil, they will not only thrive but seed around

florindae This heavily scented plant likes wetter soils. Drooping, primrose-yellow flowers form a cluster at the top of tall, light-green stems above soft-green leaves. June to July. **H × S** 60cm × 30cm. AGM

Gold-laced Group Held in clusters, the flowers are a delight with deep-maroon to almost-black petals that are finely edged in yellow. Seed-raised plants, however, may be rather varied. All have upright stems above a rosette of mid-green leaves. April to June. **H × S** 25cm × 15cm

japonica **'Miller's Crimson'** A really colourful candelabra primula with whorls of single, pink-crimson flowers carried at intervals up straight, felted, grey stems. June to July. **H × S** 60cm × 30cm. AGM

vulgaris (Common primrose) When our wild primrose displays its cheerful, soft-yellow flowers, we know spring has arrived. You may find plants on sale raised from over-cultivated forms. These have none of the simple innocence of the wild plant. April to June. **H × S** 15cm × 23cm. AGM

Potentilla 'William Rollison'

Potentilla 'Yellow Queen'

Primula florindae

Primula Gold-laced Group

Primula japonica 'Miller's Crimson'

Primula vulgaris

Prunella grandiflora 'Alba'

Prunella grandiflora 'Loveliness'

Pulmonaria 'Barfield Regalia'

Pulmonaria 'Blue Ensign'

Pulmonaria 'Diana Clare'

Pulmonaria mollis

PRUNELLA (Self heal)

These rather discreet, yet free-flowering ground-cover plants are useful for the front of a shady border. Short, stumpy spikes of large, hooded flowers are carried for many weeks above a thick carpet of long, mid-green leaves.

Needs Well-drained soil that remains moist in sun, partial shade, or shade
Great for Front of the border
Bees & Butterflies Bees
For Cutting No
Care Trouble free

grandiflora **'Alba'** This white-flowered variety forms a neat carpet. June to August. **H × S** 15cm × 45cm

grandiflora **'Loveliness'** A pretty plant with soft-lilac flowers and dense foliage. June to August. **H × S** 15cm × 45cm

PULMONARIA (Lungwort)

A spring delight and one of the earliest perennial to bloom. Sprays of funnel-shaped flowers cluster on top of stout stems above a thick, flat rosette or mound of large, often spotted, decorative leaves. As the season progresses, the leafy clump fills out.

Needs Well-drained soil that remains moist in sun, partial shade, or shade
Great for Front of the border
Bees & Butterflies Bees
For Cutting No
Care Trouble free

'Barfield Regalia' Small clusters of pink flowers open early in the season from violet-blue buds above plain-green leaves. March to April. **H × S** 45cm × 30cm

'Blue Ensign' Bright violet-blue flowers set in almost-black bracts are carried above smooth, deep-green leaves. March to April. **H × S** 25cm × 23cm. AGM

'Diana Clare' A flat rosette of long, silvery-green leaves is topped with small clusters of violet-blue flowers on lax stems. March to May. **H × S** 30cm × 30cm. AGM

mollis An easy plant to grow. Clusters of funnel-shaped, violet-blue flowers open from pink buds, forming a mist above a mound of smooth, mid-green leaves. March to April. **H × S** 45cm × 45cm

'Opal' A big, upright clump of long, broad, evenly spotted leaves throws up strong stems of soft sky-blue flowers. March to April. **H × S** 25cm × 30cm

rubra **'Bowles's Red'** This short, spreading plant has evergreen, plain-green leaves and small clusters of attractive, coral-red flowers. March to April. **H × S** 30cm × 30cm

saccharata **'Leopard'** Reddish-pink bells fading to mauve are held on short stems above fresh-green leaves, spotted with silver. March to April. **H × S** 30cm × 30cm

saccharata **'Mrs Moon'** A free-flowering variety with pure-blue flowers that emerge from pink buds. It forms a neatly rounded mound of silver-spotted, mid-green leaves. March to April. **H × S** 30cm × 30cm

'Sissinghurst White' Pure-white flowers sit in airy clusters above silver-splashed, pale-green leaves on this slowly spreading plant. Can be slow to establish. March to April. **H × S** 30cm × 30cm. AGM

'Trevi Fountain' Dense clusters of large, open, mid-blue flowers emerge from violet buds. These are carried well above silver-splashed, dark green leaves. April to May. **H × S** 35cm × 30cm

RHODIOLA (Rose root)

rosea Looking something like a sedum, this handsome little plant evolves through the season. In early spring hummocks of short stems are thickly clothed with evenly spaced, fleshy, grey leaves that resemble scales. These terminate in a cluster of tiny, lime-green flowers that will later become fluffy with stamens. The stems then stretch upwards forming a loose mound. It is easily tucked among other perennials. May to June. **H × S** 30cm × 30cm

Needs Well-drained soil in sun
Great for Front of the border
Bees & Butterflies Bees
For Cutting No
Care Extremely tolerant of a wide variety of conditions. Plant and leave it alone

Pulmonaria 'Opal'

Pulmonaria rubra 'Bowles's Red'

Pulmonaria saccharata 'Leopard'

Pulmonaria saccharata 'Mrs Moon'

Pulmonaria 'Sissinghurst White'

Pulmonaria 'Trevi Fountain'

Rhodiola rosea

Rodgersia sambucifolia

Rudbeckia laciniata 'Herbstsonne'

RODGERSIA

sambucifolia A striking plant for damp spots. Curling sprays of tiny, cream flowers are carried on side branches down tall, strong, red stems. The bold leaves resemble those of the horse-chestnut tree. July.
H × S 90cm × 80cm

Needs Moist soil in sun or partial shade
Great for Damp soils: bogs, pond edges, or by a stream
Bees & Butterflies Bees
For Cutting No
Care Trouble free in the right soil

RUDBECKIA (Black-eyed Susan)

Brightly coloured, easy to grow, and cheerful, these daisies have distinctive cone-shaped centres. They are invaluable for late-summer and autumn colour, forming broad mounds or upright clumps covered with flowers for many weeks.

Needs Well-drained soil in sun
Great for Middle and back of the border
Bees & Butterflies Yes
For Cutting Yes
Care Trouble free and needs no staking

***fulgida* var. *sullivantii* 'Goldsturm'** Large, black-centred, golden-yellow flowers are carried on a broad, upright dome. July to October. **H × S** 90cm × 80cm. AGM

***laciniata* 'Herbstsonne'** Ideal for the back of a border, this tall, imposing plant has green-centred, citrus-yellow flowers. August to September. **H × S** 180cm × 105cm. AGM

triloba An airy, upright plant with smallish, round, black-centred, rich-yellow flowers on slender, leafy, branched stems. August to October. **H × S** 90cm × 75cm. AGM

Rudbeckia fulgida var. *sullivantii* 'Goldsturm'

Rudbeckia triloba

SALVIA (Sage)

There really should be a place in every garden for these long- and free-flowering plants. Neat and mounding, then getting bigger as the season trundles on, they are perfect for mixing with other perennials. The tiny flowers are carried in slender spikes up stems that are sparingly covered with leaves. These look distinctly sage-like, but their fragrance is not as pleasant when they are crushed between the fingers.

Needs Well-drained soil in sun
Great for Front or middle of the border
Bees & Butterflies Bees
For Cutting Yes
Care Trouble free. Cut back after blooming to encourage further flowers

nemorosa **'Amethyst'** An upright plant with slim, rather wavy spikes of tiny, amethyst-pink flowers and mid-green leaves. June to August. **H × S** 60cm × 45cm. AGM

nemorosa **'Caradonna'** The slender, firmly upright, purple stems carry spikes of small, blue-purple flowers and grey-green leaves. This makes an attractive and quite airy plant. June to August. **H × S** 50cm × 45cm. AGM

nemorosa **'Ostfriesland'** A bushy plant with spikes of violet flowers emerging from mauve calyces. June to August. **H × S** 60cm × 45cm. AGM

× *sylvestris* 'Blauhügel' This is a shorter, compact variety with lavender-blue flower spikes, and is ideal for planting at the front of the border. June to August. **H × S** 45cm × 45cm. AGM

Salvia nemorosa 'Amethyst'

Salvia nemorosa 'Caradonna'

Salvia nemorosa 'Ostfriesland'

Salvia × *sylvestris* 'Blauhügel'

Salvia × *sylvestris* 'Schneehügel'

Salvia × *sylvestris* 'Mainacht'

Salvia verticillata 'Purple Rain'

Sanguisorba menziesii

× *sylvestris* **'Mainacht'** Tiny, violet-blue flowers are carried in slender spikes and the plant forms a neat, round mound. June to August. **H × S** 70cm × 45cm. AGM

× *sylvestris* **'Schneehügel'** A short plant with spikes of white flowers and light-green leaves. It blooms for many weeks. June to August. **H × S** 45cm × 45cm

verticillata **'Purple Rain'** This salvia is a little different in that its small purple flowers are carried in even whorls up the stem. They rise above mid-green, deeply serrated leaves and the plant makes a spreading clump. There is also a creamy-white form, *S. verticillata* 'Alba'. June to August. **H × S** 60cm × 60cm

SANGUISORBA (Burnet)

With their slim stems topped by poker-like flowers, burnets are graceful plants with a 'see-through' quality that makes them invaluable mixers in the border. Some flowers change as the stamens emerge and turn fluffy, like catkins or bottle brushes. The deeply divided leaves are highly decorative.

Needs Well-drained soil that remains moist in sun or partial shade
Great for Front, middle, or back of the border
Bees & Butterflies Bees
For Cutting Yes
Care Cut back to the first set of leaves after blooming to encourage more flowers. *S. tenuifolia* types die back early, so cut them right to the ground

menziesii A handsome plant with fat spikes of maroon flowers that soften in colour as the stamens appear. The lovely grey-green leaves are tinted red. July to September. **H × S** 75cm × 60cm

obtusa Long, shaggy, bright-pink 'catkins' arch gently at the top above a clump of deeply divided, mid-green leaves. July to September. **H × S** 75cm × 60cm

officinalis (Great burnet) A very tall, elegant plant with compact, burgundy flower spikes carried above long, deeply divided leaves. It sometimes suffers from mildew. July to September. **H × S** 150cm × 30cm

officinalis **'Red Thunder'** Small, dense heads of rich-red flowers are held above a carpet of small, mid-green leaves. July to September. **H × S** 30cm × 60cm

'Pink Tanna' Above a spreading mound of deeply divided leaves, long, pink 'pokers' rise up on elegant, willowy stems. July to September. **H × S** 60cm × 75cm

stipulata A stiffly upright plant with fluffy, white flowers and long, serrated leaves. July to September. **H × S** 90cm × 65cm

tenuifolia var. alba Emerging on upright stems, the long, slender, white flower spikes arch slightly as they age. They are carried above a dense mound of soft-green leaves. July to September. **H × S** 150cm × 75cm

tenuifolia 'Pink Elephant' A graceful plant with long, slender, rich-pink flowers carried above divided grey-green leaves. Ideal for the back of a border. July to September. **H × S** 150cm × 75cm

Sanguisorba officinalis 'Red Thunder'

Sanguisorba 'Pink Tanna'

Sanguisorba obtusa
with *Stachys byzantina* 'Big Ears'

Sanguisorba officinalis

Sanguisorba stipulata

Sanguisorba tenuifolia var. *alba*

Sanguisorba tenuifolia 'Pink Elephant'

Saxifraga × urbium

Scabiosa 'Butterfly Blue'

Scabiosa caucasica 'Clive Greaves'

Scabiosa caucasica 'Miss Willmott'

Scabiosa columbaria subsp. *ochroleuca*

Scabiosa lucida

SAXIFRAGA (London pride)

× **urbium** Grown in gardens for around 300 years, this robust plant often lines the edges of paths. With pretty, pale-pink flowers and evergreen foliage that slowly forms a broad mat of round, mid-green leaves, it is a faultless ground-covering plant. May to June. **H × S** 45cm × 60cm. AGM

Needs Well-drained soil in sun or partial shade
Great for Very front of the border
Bees & Butterflies Bees
For Cutting Yes
Care Trouble free

SCABIOSA (Scabious)

A disc-like centre surrounded by a frill of petals gives the flowers a rather dignified look. Nectar-rich, they are carried on slender stems, above a clump of deeply divided, mid-green leaves, over a long period.

Needs Well-drained soil in sun
Great for Front, middle, or back of the border
Bees & Butterflies Yes
For Cutting Yes
Care Cut back after blooming to encourage further flowers. Very floriferous, so may be short-lived, and can also suffer from mildew

'Butterfly Blue' A good variety for containers, with short stems of soft-blue flowers that attract butterflies. June to September. **H × S** 30cm × 30cm

caucasica **'Clive Greaves'** At one time, this was a popular plant in the cut-flower industry. The large, soft-blue flowers are carried on long, slender stems. June to September. **H × S** 60cm × 30cm. AGM *caucasica* **'Miss Willmott'** The large, milk-white flowers with pin-cushion centres are wonderful for cutting. June to September. **H × S** 60cm × 30cm. AGM

columbaria **subsp.** *ochroleuca* This free-flowering variety with small, lemon blooms makes bushy swathes. An excellent plant for the wilder garden, it seeds freely. June to September. **H × S** 45cm × 60cm

lucida Possessing similar qualities to *S. columbaria*, this variety is more suited to a drier soil. The flowers are small and lavender-blue and the leaves silver-green. June to September. **H × S** 60cm × 30cm

SEDUM (Ice plant)

Succulent by nature and in appearance, the border varieties of this easily grown, bee- and butterfly-attracting group need little attention. Fresh grey-green foliage emerges in spring and is followed by plate-like flower heads on stout stems that, when dry, give handsome structure to the winter border.

Needs Well-drained soil in sun
Great for Front or middle of the border
Bees & Butterflies Yes
For Cutting Yes
Care Trouble free. Some varieties with broad heads may topple over, especially in richer soils. Cut back the stems in late spring to create a shorter, more compact plant.

'Abbey Dore' Neatly domed heads of pale-pink flowers deepen in colour as they age. The short stems form a round clump that tends to splay outwards in good soil, so divide every few years, or pinch out the early buds to keep the stems short. August to October. **H × S** 45cm × 60cm

'Bertram Anderson' A prostrate plant with round, purplish leaves and arching stems with open clusters of tiny, rich-red flowers. It might take a year or two to establish. August to October. **H × S** 23cm × 30cm. AGM

(Herbstfreude Group) 'Herbstfreude' Also known as 'Autumn Joy', this popular variety makes a sturdy clump. Pale-green foliage is topped with broad, gently domed heads of tiny, lime-green buds that open into coral-pink, then dark pink stars. August to October. **H × S** 60cm × 45cm. AGM

'Matrona' Upright stems in eye-catching deep maroon bear broad heads of small, soft rose-pink flowers on this very handsome plant. The dark green leaves are also tinted maroon. August to October. **H × S** 60cm × 45cm. AGM

Sedum 'Abbey Dore'

Sedum 'Bertram Anderson'

Sedum (Herbstfreude Group) 'Herbstfreude'

Sedum 'Matrona'

Sedum 'Red Cauli'

Sedum spectabile

Sedum telephium (Atropurpureum Group)
'Purple Emperor'

Sedum telephium (Atropurpureum Group)
'Xenox'

Selinum wallichianum

Senecio polyodon

'Mr Goodbud' A lovely new introduction with big heads of large, starry flowers that open pink-mauve and deepen to a rich red-mauve. The blue-green of the stems and leaves makes a wonderful contrast. July to October. **H × S** 30cm × 30cm. AGM

'Red Cauli' This richly coloured variety bears small, domed heads of flowers in an intense shade of red. Both stems and leaves are dark red. July to October. **H × S** 30cm × 30cm. AGM

spectabile Held in small, flat clusters, the soft-pink flowers become fluffy as they age. The foliage is a pale green and forms a sturdy, upright mound. August to October. **H × S** 45cm × 45cm. AGM

telephium (**Atropurpureum Group**) **'Purple Emperor'** The upright, purple-brown stems and leaves are topped with small, rounded clusters of pale-pink flowers. The darker bracts remain after the flowers fade. August to October. **H × S** 60cm × 45cm. AGM

telephium (**Atropurpureum Group**) **'Xenox'** An excellent variety, this creates a neat, dusky-purple mound that looks good all season. Flat heads of tiny, red flowers bloom above the foliage. August to October. **H × S** 30cm × 30cm. AGM

SELINUM

wallichianum Beautifully structured with broad heads of tiny, white flowers, this plant looks similar to our native cow parsley. The dusky-red stems emerge from a dense mound of deeply divided, mid-green leaves that, although large, have a delicate quality. July to September. **H × S** 120cm × 90cm

Needs Well-drained soil in sun or partial shade
Great for Middle of the border
Bees & Butterflies Bees
For Cutting No
Care Prefers a soil that does not dry out, otherwise easy to grow and will self-seed

SENECIO

polyodon Grow this charming plant between perennials with dense foliage, where its wispiness will have a softening effect. The small, bright-pink daisies rise above a rosette of fresh-green leaves. June to September. **H × S** 30cm × 30cm

Needs Well-drained soil; sun or partial shade
Great for Front of the border
Bees & Butterflies Bees
For Cutting Yes
Care Likely to be short-lived, but may seed around. Otherwise trouble free

Sedum 'Mr Goodbud' (front) and *Sedum* (Herbstfreude Group) 'Herbstfreude' (behind) with
Persicaria affinis 'Darjeeling Red' and *Echinacea purpurea* 'White Swan'

Sidalcea 'Brilliant'

Sidalcea candida

Sidalcea 'Elsie Heugh'

SIDALCEA (Prairie mallow)

Paper-thin flowers are carried around the stems of these pretty plants that resemble a short hollyhock. The flower spikes vary in height, eventually growing into a neat, uneven, upright clump with delicate, shiny, deeply divided leaves.

Needs Well-drained soil in sun
Great for Front or middle of the border
Bees & Butterflies Yes
For Cutting Yes
Care Trouble free. Just cut back after flowering to increase longevity

'Brilliant' The pink-red flowers are carried on shorter stems than other varieties, making this ideal for smaller gardens. July to August. **H × S** 80cm × 45cm

candida Pure-white flowers sometimes with gaps between the petals, are loosely spaced along the spikes of this attractive variety. It is usually seed grown, so forms may vary. July to August. **H × S** 90cm × 45cm

'Elsie Heugh' A very pretty plant with soft-pink flowers that are neatly fringed around the edges of the petals. July to August. **H × S** 90cm × 45cm. AGM

Stachys byzantina

Stachys byzantina 'Silver Carpet'

Stachys macrantha

STACHYS

Within this group there are two distinct types: one has semi-evergreen, woolly, silver-grey foliage that is soft to the touch, the other has plain, mid-green leaves. The woolly-leaved varieties add texture and make extremely useful ground-cover at the front of a border. Those with green leaves are more upright in habit and better for the middle of a border. All have funnel-shaped flowers with large lower lips.

Needs Well-drained soil in sun or partial shade
Great for Front or middle of the border
Bees & Butterflies Bees
For Cutting Yes
Care Trouble free, but *S. byzantina* types will benefit from a trim to get rid of the old woody stems. In warm summers the leaves may get a mild attack of mildew

byzantina (Lamb's ears) From a carpet of silver-grey, furry leaves, numerous soft, grey stems bear tiny, pink flowers, which emerge from woolly buds. June to August. **H × S** 45cm × 60cm

byzantina **'Big Ears'** As the name suggests, the felted, silver-grey leaves of this variety are very big. The long, leafy stems carry woolly whorls of tiny, lilac-pink flowers. June to August. **H × S** 60cm × 60cm

byzantina **'Silver Carpet'** Rarely producing any flowers, this plant forms a perfect carpet of furry, silver leaves that is so dense, weeds find it almost impossible to penetrate. June to August. **H × S** 30cm × 60cm

macrantha (Big-sage) Big spikes of large, purple, trumpet-shaped flowers are carried on thick, upright stems, but soon fade. The foliage forms rounded clumps, which contrast well with frothy plants. July to August. **H × S** 70cm × 45cm

officinalis **'Hummelo'** (Betony) The tightly packed spikes of this compact, upright plant are an unusual shade of rosy-purple. They are carried on straight, sparsely leaved stems above a rosette of long, serrated, mid-green leaves. July to August. **H × S** 45cm × 30cm

officinalis **'Rosea'** Very neat and upright in habit, this pretty variety has stiff stems that carry short, stumpy spikes of little, pale-pink flowers above mid-green leaves. July to August. **H × S** 40cm × 30cm

Stachys officinalis 'Hummelo'

Stachys officinalis 'Rosea'

Stachys byzantina 'Big Ears' with *Eryngium × zabelii* 'Big Blue'

Stemmacantha centaureoides

Stipa arundinacea

Stipa calamagrostis

Stipa gigantea

Stokesia laevis

Stokesia laevis 'Alba'

STEMMACANTHA

centaureoides This striking plant may at first prove difficult to establish. Once settled, it produces globular heads of fluffy flowers set in scaly, bronze cups. Serrated-edged, silver leaves form a basal clump. Formerly listed as *Centaurea* 'Pulchra Major'. July to August. **H × S** 90cm × 60cm

Needs Well-drained, fairly moist soil, in sun
Great for Middle of the border
Bees & Butterflies Yes
For Cutting Yes
Care Once established, trouble free

STIPA

Handsome and deservedly popular, these grasses send up thick tufts of fine leaves and fountains of elegant flowers that are easy to blend into a border.

Needs Well-drained soil in a warm spot in sun
Great for Front or back of a border
Bees & Butterflies No
For Cutting Yes
Care Reasonably trouble free. Shorter varieties may seed about once established

arundinacea (also listed as *Anemanthele lessoniana*) Arching tufts of very fine, mid-green leaves turn a striking orange-bronze as the season progresses. Small, purple flowers are borne on wispy stems. August to September. **H × S** 50cm × 45cm

calamagrostis White flowers in soft, silky, feathery plumes emerge from a clump of mid-green leaves. Reliable, even in poor soils. June to October. **H × S** 90cm × 75cm

gigantea Very tall and very handsome, the stiff stems of soft-beige, oat-like flowers form airy plumes that catch the light. August to September. **H × S** 180cm × 120cm. AGM

STOKESIA (Stokes's aster)

When these plants get their roots down and start to bloom, the big, flat, flowers with fringed petals are really eye-catching. Their stiff stems spring from a rosette of long, leathery, evergreen leaves.

Needs Well-drained soil that does not dry out in sun or partial shade
Great for Front of the border
Bees & Butterflies Yes
For Cutting Yes
Care May take a little while to establish. Trouble free, especially in a slightly acid soil

laevis Lilac-blue flowers bloom over several weeks. July to October. **H × S** 60cm × 50cm

laevis **'Alba'** A plant with creamy-white flowers, often flushed with very pale lilac. July to October. **H × S** 60cm × 50cm

SUCCISA (Devil's bit scabious)

pratensis This very free-flowering plant is a magnet for bees and butterflies. Forming a 'see-through' network, the fine, branched stems terminate in a compact ball of lilac-blue flowers, like bright pom-poms. July to October. **H × S** 120cm × 90cm

Needs Well-drained soil in sun or partial shade
Great for Middle of a border
Bees & Butterflies Yes
For Cutting Yes
Care Will self-seed once established but is not invasive

SYMPHYTUM (Comfrey)

Although its rough foliage may look rather coarse, comfrey will shade the ground so thoroughly that weeds get smothered. The flowers are carried in small clusters on long stems. Some varieties spread rapidly and uncontrollably; others are well behaved.

Needs Any soil that does not dry out in sun, partial shade, or shade
Great for Wild areas
Bees & Butterflies Bees
For Cutting No
Care Trouble free

azureum The intense colour of its bright sky-blue flowers is very desirable, but this creeping variety should be grown with caution. May to July. **H × S** 45cm × 90cm

'Hidcote Pink' Short stems of nodding, soft-blue and pale-pink flowers sit above a well-behaved, dense carpet of leaves. May to July. **H × S** 45cm × 90cm

'Rubrum' A handsome, non-invasive plant with crimson flowers and dark green leaves. May to June. **H × S** 30cm × 45cm

× uplandicum (Russian comfrey) Clusters of blue, purple, or violet flowers are carried on long, leafy stems. Robust and long flowering, it is generally grown from seed. May to September. **H × S** 90cm × 90cm

TELLIMA (Fringe cups)

***grandiflora* 'Forest Frost'** Unassuming yet invaluable for ground-cover, this evergreen plant bears slender spikes of dainty, green bells, fringed around the edges with pink. The vine-like foliage starts out bright green; by autumn it is burnished with bronze. May to July. **H × S** 60cm × 45cm

Needs Well-drained soil in partial shade
Great for Shady spots
Bees & Butterflies Bees
For Cutting Yes
Care Trouble free

Succisa pratensis

Symphytum azureum

Symphytum 'Hidcote Pink'

Symphytum 'Rubrum'

Symphytum × *uplandicum*

Tellima grandiflora 'Forest Frost'

Thalictrum 'Black Stockings'

Thalictrum delavayi

Thalictrum delavayi 'Hewitt's Double'

Thalictrum 'Elin'

Thalictrum flavum 'Illuminator'

Thalictrum rochebruneanum

THALICTRUM (Meadow rue)

Tall and very elegant, these delightful perennials will light up a shady part of the garden for weeks with their delicate sprays of tiny, cup-shaped flowers. The individual blooms are single or semi-double and are borne on the side branches of straight stems. They are held well above deeply divided, fern-like foliage that remains attractive right through to late autumn.

Needs Soil that remains moist in partial sun or dappled shade
Great for Borders and woodland
Bees & Butterflies Bees
For Cutting Yes
Care Trouble free in the right soil. Although sturdy, *T. delavayi* and *T. flavum* may need staking in a windy spot.

'Black Stockings' Aptly named, this plant has particularly dark, long, purple-black stems. In spring, they rise up from a clump of delicate, mid-green leaves and carry heads of fluffy, rose-purple flowers in summer. June to July. **H × S** 90cm × 75cm

delavayi Open sprays of small flowers in a delicate lavender with cream stamens are carried on soft-mauve stems. There is also a lovely, pure-white form, *T. delavayi* 'Album'. June to August. **H × S** 150cm × 75cm. AGM

delavayi **'Hewitt's Double'** As the name suggests, this is a double form, but it can be tricky to establish. Once settled, the airy sprays of small, mauve, pom-pom flowers are both long-lasting and exquisite. June to August. **H × S** 150cm × 75cm. AGM

'Elin' In spring, the handsome, blue-grey foliage of this variety displays a red tint, which has faded by the time the open sprays of lilac flowers emerge. This beautiful giant of a plant needs no staking. June to August. **H × S** 180cm × 90cm

flavum **'Illuminator'** The brilliant-yellow leaves turn a soft blue-green as spring advances. Towards the top of tall, well-branched stems, clusters of fluffy, soft-yellow flowers appear. June to July. **H × S** 180cm × 75cm

rochebruneanum A robust, tall variety with sprays of open, shallow-cupped, lavender flowers with pale-yellow stamens. These are carried on soft-purple stems above handsome, deeply divided, mid-green leaves. June to August. **H × S** 150cm × 75cm

THERMOPSIS (False lupin)

lanceolata Resembling a slender, yellow lupin, this neat, clump-forming plant has similar pea-shaped flowers. They are carried in open spikes on almost-black stems with green foliage that is reminiscent of the leaves of false indigo (*Baptisia*). May to June. **H × S** 90cm × 75cm

Needs Well-drained soil in sun
Great for Middle of the border
Bees & Butterflies No
For Cutting No
Care Slow to establish, but can be left undisturbed for years

TIARELLA (Foam flower)

cordifolia This pretty woodlander forms domes of evergreen, vine-like foliage that will, in time, creep over the ground to form a dense mat. The starry, white flowers are borne in airy spikes just above the mound of leaves, which turn shades of red in autumn. April to May. **H × S** 30cm × 60cm. AGM

Needs Humus-rich, moist soil in partial shade
Great for Shady areas
Bees & Butterflies No
For Cutting Yes
Care Can suffer attack by vine weevil

TRADESCANTIA (Spiderwort)

A thicket of grassy leaves is topped, in early summer, with clusters of flat, three-petalled blooms that flower over a long period. In the centre is a fluffy tuft from which the long, pollen-tipped stamens protrude.

Needs Moist soil in sun or partial shade
Great for Front of the border
Bees & Butterflies No
For Cutting Yes
Care The leaves can be prone to leaf spot in the sun. If they become marked, trim them back, which also promotes more flowers

(Andersoniana Group) 'Concord Grape' The combination of soft-purple flowers and disease-resistant, grey-green leaves is lovely. June to August. **H × S** 45cm × 60cm

(Andersoniana Group) 'J. C. Weguelin' A free-flowering plant with blooms of soft violet-blue and fresh-green leaves. June to August. **H × S** 45cm × 60cm

(Andersoniana Group) 'Osprey' Pure-white flowers are enhanced by a centre of fluffy, blue stamens. June to August. **H × S** 45cm × 60cm

(Andersoniana Group) 'Perrine's Pink' A taller variety with a pretty mix of lilac-pink flowers and grey-green, disease-resistant leaves. June to August. **H × S** 60cm × 70cm

Thermopsis lanceolata

Tiarella cordifolia

Tradescantia (Andersoniana Group) 'Concord Grape'

Tradescantia (Andersoniana Group) 'J. C. Weguelin'

Tradescantia (Andersoniana Group) 'Osprey'

Tradescantia (Andersoniana Group) 'Perrine's Pink'

Tricyrtis formosana 'Dark Beauty'

Tricyrtis hirta 'Miyazaki'

Tricyrtis hirta 'Taiwan Atrianne'

Tricyrtis 'Tojen'

Trifolium rubens

TRICYRTIS (Toad lily)

Exotic and intriguing, these very late-flowering woodland plants will, given the right soil, slowly spread. At each leaf joint, the upright or arching stems carry a smallish, star-shaped flower, often spotted inside. Its six waxy petals are cupped around a raised 'mast' that looks rather like the blades of a helicopter and bristles with tiny beads of nectar.

Needs Soil that remains moist in partial shade or shade
Great for Shady areas
Bees & Butterflies No
For Cutting No
Care Trouble free if planted where they are not competing with other border plants

formosana **'Dark Beauty'** The many forms of *T. formosana* have mid-green leaves and their white flowers are heavily dotted with purple. On this tall plant, the spots are so closely set the petals look almost mauve. September to October. **H × S** 90cm × 50cm

hirta **'Miyazaki'** Lightly speckled with purple, the eye-catching white flowers appear at the upper leaf joints on upright stems. The leaves are large, dark green, and deeply grooved. September to October. **H × S** 75cm × 70cm

hirta **'Taiwan Atrianne'** The white flowers of this upright, leafy plant are sparsely speckled with maroon. Given a shady spot with really moist soil, this will grow tall and add autumn impact. September to October. **H × S** 105cm × 60cm

'Tojen' A sprawling plant with long, arching stems of white flowers. The petal edges are delicately tinged with lilac. August to September. **H × S** 75cm × 60cm

TRIFOLIUM (Clover)

rubens Although clovers can be invasive, this upright bushy form is not. The pink-red flowers form neat, tapering 'towers' that look fluffy when the individual blooms emerge. These are carried on sturdy, bright-green stems with long leaves. June to August. **H × S** 60cm × 45cm

Needs Well-drained soil that stays moist in sun or partial shade
Great for Front or middle of the border. Works well in containers
Bees & Butterflies Bees
For Cutting No
Care Cut the plant back to keep it tidy and to encourage a few more flowers. Tends to be short-lived, but you may find self-sown seedlings around the base

TRILLIUM (Wake robin)

These select, slow-growing plants are best suited to dappled shade beneath deciduous trees and large shrubs. Their structure is very unusual, but beautiful: petals, bracts, and leaves are all in groups of three.

Needs Soil that remains moist in partial shade
Great for Woodland
Bees & Butterflies Bees
For Cutting No
Care Slow to get going. If possible, buy big plants, which will establish better

luteum (Yellow trillium) Carried on thick stems, the long, soft-lemon, scented flowers sit on top of large leaves that are heavily mottled with khaki. It will not thrive in acid soils. April to May. **H × S** 30cm × 30cm. AGM

sessile (Sessile trillium) A mounding plant with large, mid-green leaves, slightly blotched with darker tones. These form a 'plate' for the upright, burgundy flowers. Will flourish under trees where the soil is rich in leaf mould. April to May. **H × S** 30cm × 30cm

UVULARIA (Merrybells)

grandiflora An attractive plant for a lightly shaded spot with slender, soft-yellow bells that droop from branched stems. A little slow to get going, but will slowly spread. April to May. **H × S** 60cm × 30cm. AGM

Needs Soil that remains moist in partial shade
Great for Woodland
Bees & Butterflies Bees
For Cutting No
Care Prefers ground rich in leaf mould

VALERIANA (Valerian)

Flat heads of beautifully, scented, tiny, white flowers are held on upright stems that rise from a thick clump of attractive foliage. A good choice for a naturalistic planting.

Needs Soil that remains moist in sun or partial shade
Great for Middle or back of the border
Bees & Butterflies Bees
For Cutting No
Care Trouble free, but cats will roll in it

officinalis (Common valerian) Tall and very upright stems with deeply divided foliage bear domed sprays of tiny, white flowers. July to August. **H × S** 150cm × 60cm

phu **'Aurea'** A tufted clump of bright-yellow leaves turns green by summer, when domed sprays of small, white, honey-scented flowers appear. May to June. **H × S** 60cm × 45cm

Trillium luteum

Trillium sessile

Uvularia grandiflora

Valeriana phu 'Aurea'

Valeriana officinalis

Verbascum chaixii 'Album' in front of red *Persicaria amplexicaulis* 'Taurus'

VERBASCUM (Mullein)

For flowers with impact and vertical structure, few plants can match mulleins. Tall, elegant spikes of usually single flowers open over many weeks and are carried above a rosette of broad leaves. Most are short-lived, but the varieties below should survive two or three years, maybe more.

Needs Well-drained soil in sun or partial shade
Great for Middle or back of the border
Bees & Butterflies Bees
For Cutting Yes
Care Varieties grown from seed will reproduce easily, so if you want to keep numbers down and aid longevity, remember to dead-head them

chaixii **'Album'** A plant reliably raised from seed, it bears slim spikes of pure-white flowers with purple stamens. Carried on sturdy stems above a rosette of mid-green leaves, they bloom for many weeks. June to August. **H × S** 90cm × 55cm

(Cotswold Group) 'Gainsborough' Large flowers in a pretty soft-yellow bloom on thick, grey-green stems that rise above a flat rosette of grey-green leaves. June to August. **H × S** 120cm × 60cm. AGM

olympicum A dramatic and defiant plant that throws up candelabras of bright-yellow flowers. The stiff stems have many side branches and large, soft-green leaves. July to August. **H × S** 180cm × 75cm

phoeniceum **'Violetta'** A slender plant with a wispy quality. The deep-violet flowers are carried at wide intervals up slender stems above shiny, dark green leaves. June to August. **H × S** 75cm × 30cm

Verbascum (Cotswold Group) 'Gainsborough'

Verbascum olympicum

Verbascum phoeniceum 'Violetta'

VERBENA

The slender, branched stems add height to the border and create a lovely 'see-through' effect. Although rather short-lived, they produce masses of tiny, bright flowers that are loved by insects.

Needs Well-drained soil in sun
Great for Middle or back of the border
Bees & Butterflies Yes
For Cutting Yes
Care Easy to grow. Allow the plant to seed around and hope for seedlings

bonariensis A tall, elegant plant with rigid, sparsely leaved, well-branched stems. These are topped with small clusters of tiny, violet flowers over a long period. June to October. **H × S** 120cm × 45cm. AGM

hastata **f.** *rosea* Tiny pink flowers emerge from deep-pink buds at the top of stems that branch profusely towards the top. Easier to establish than *V. bonariensis*. June to October. **H × S** 110cm × 45cm. AGM

VERONICA (Speedwell)

These charming plants form either a neat mound or a spreading carpet and send up masses of short flower spikes. The simply shaped blooms add welcome colour, with *spicata* types flowering over a long period.

Needs Well-drained soil in sun or partial shade
Great for Front or middle of the border
Bees & Butterflies Bees
For Cutting Yes
Care *Gentianoides* types prefer soil that does not dry out. Cut back flowering stems of the others to encourage better growth

'Ellen Mae' One of our own introductions, this was selected for the unusual colour of the short, lilac-pink flower spikes. Its small, mid-green leaves create a low mound. May to June. **H × S** 30cm × 30cm

gentianoides Slender, open spikes of lovely, sky-blue flowers appear in late spring. They are carried above a tight, spreading carpet of shiny, deep-green leaves. May to June. **H × S** 45cm × 60cm

'Shirley Blue' A domed mound of mid-green leaves is covered with short spikes of flowers in a vivid shade of blue. This speedwell flowers over a long period. May to July. **H × S** 30cm × 30cm. AGM

spicata Pretty, tapering spires of tiny, mid-blue flowers are carried in generous quantities on stiff stems. The long leaves are serrated. Seed grown, so can vary in height. June to September. **H × S** 30–90cm × 30cm

Verbena bonariensis

Verbena hastata f. *rosea*

Veronica 'Ellen Mae'

Veronica gentianoides

Veronica 'Shirley Blue'

Veronica spicata

Veronica spicata 'Icicle'

Veronica spicata 'Rotfuchs'

spicata **'Icicle'** A short, broad, mounding plant with neat spikes of clean, pure-white flowers and long, grey-green leaves. June to September. **H × S** 30cm × 45cm

spicata **'Rotfuchs'** The bright red-pink spikes are carried above a slowly creeping mound of long, mid-green leaves. June to September. **H × S** 30cm × 30cm

VERONICASTRUM (Culver's root)

Perfectly architectural in form, these perennials look stunning when planted in drifts, adding graceful linear structure to the border. Very tall, slender, tapering flower spikes of tiny, bell-shaped flowers are carried in layers. Below each, right down to the bottom of the stem, are whorls of long, pointed leaves. The 'scaffolding' of spikes is so slim that these perennials won't hide anything planted behind them.

Needs Soil that remains moist in sun or partial shade
Great for Back of a border
Bees & Butterflies Bees
For Cutting No
Care Trouble free in the right soil

virginicum **'Album'** This beautiful variety carries long spikes of white flowers on bronze stems with dark green leaves. July to September. **H × S** 150cm × 90cm

virginicum **'Fascination'** Wands of rich-lilac flowers are held in branched tiers, rather like a candelabra, on this handsome, eye-catching plant. These become paler in colour as the blooms fade. July to September. **H × S** 150cm × 90cm

Veronicastrum virginicum 'Album'

Veronicastrum virginicum 'Fascination'

Veronicastrum virginicum 'Lavendulturm'

Veronicastrum virginicum f. *roseum* 'Pink Glow'

virginicum **'Lavendulturm'** Early to bloom, this variety has pale-lilac flower spikes and mid-green leaves. It finishes flowering before others have really got going. July to August. **H × S** 150cm × 90cm

virginicum **f.** *roseum* **'Pink Glow'** A lovely and rather subtle plant with spikes of palest pastel-pink flowers and dark green leaves. It creates a gentle, bushy structure. July to September. **H × S** 120cm × 90cm

VIOLA

These cheerful little perennials are ideal for growing at the base of other plants and some are scented. All produce large quantities of small flowers with five petals that splay outwards. They sit prettily above a tight, clump of heart-shaped leaves.

Needs Well-drained soil in sun or partial shade
Great for Front of a border
Bees & Butterflies No
For Cutting Yes
Care Trouble free; some will seed around

cornuta **'Belmont Blue'** A reliable perennial, this produces lots of quite large, lavender-blue flowers on branched stems with rich-green leaves. When happy, this will spread and drift through other plants. Cut back to keep it tidy. May to September. **H × S** 15cm × 15cm

labradorica This variety, which is ideal for dotting around the border, has reddish-purple leaves that look good long after the small, purple flowers have faded. In the right spot, it will produce seedlings. April to June. **H × S** 15cm × 15cm

'Königin Charlotte' A delightful little plant with parma violet-scented, rich-purple flowers. The tight, mound of shiny, deep-green leaves is studded with blooms in spring. February to May. **H × S** 20cm × 20cm

sororia **'Freckles'** A profusion of large, violet-speckled, white flowers springs from a dense carpet of shiny, leathery, mid-green leaves. May to June. **H × S** 30cm × 40cm

WALDSTEINIA (Golden strawberry)

ternata Excellent for ground-cover, this spreading evergreen bears single, golden-yellow flowers, like those of a strawberry. These are scattered in sprays above a clump of round, shiny, dark green leaves. April to May. **H × S** 15cm × 50cm

Needs Well-drained soil in partial shade
Great for Ground-cover
Bees & Butterflies No
For Cutting No
Care Trouble free in the right soil

Viola cornuta 'Belmont Blue'

Viola labradorica

Viola 'Königin Charlotte'

Viola sororia 'Freckles'

Waldsteinia ternata

Author's acknowledgments

Thanks to the following for their help; my husband Ric for taking on the extra nursery duties while I buried my head in this book, and for his encouragement. To Allison and Martin Walter for reading the final copy. To Clive Nichols for his generosity in letting me use his photograph. And many thanks to Sue Gordon and Anna Kruger for their knowledge, advice and enthusiastic input.